TORNADO
YORK

New-build £3million A1 Peppercorn Pacific No. 60163 *Tornado* stands at York station with the return leg of the 'Scarborough Flyer' on June 4, 2016. A major crowd puller, *Tornado* has captured the public imagination in the 21st century in the same way as did the classic locomotives of the steam era. ROBIN JONES

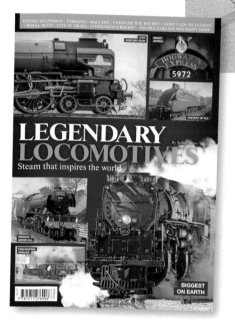

COVER PICTURE: Union Pacific Big Boy 4-8-8-4 No. 4014 has returned to steam nearly 60 years after its final revenue-earning service, and is seen arriving at Odgen Union station in Utah on May 9, 2019, to take part in major celebrations to mark the 150th anniversary of the First Transcontinental Railroad. UNION PACIFIC

COVER INSETS: Peppercorn A1 Pacific No. 60163 *Tornado*; GWR 4-6-0 No. 5972 *Olton Hall* as *Hogwarts Castle*; LNER A4 Pacific No. 4468 *Mallard*; LNER A3 Pacific No. 60103 *Flying Scotsman*; and Ffestiniog Railway double Fairlie *Merddin Emrys*.

AUTHOR:
Robin Jones

PRODUCTION EDITOR:
Nigel Devereux

DESIGN:
Craig Lamb
Kriele Ltd
design_lamb@btinternet.com

COVER DESIGN:
Michael Baumber

PUBLISHER:
Steve O'Hara

ADVERTISING MANAGER:
Sue Keily
skeily@mortons.co.uk

PUBLISHING DIRECTOR:
Dan Savage

MARKETING MANAGER:
Charlotte Park
cpark@mortons.co.uk

COMMERCIAL DIRECTOR:
Nigel Hole

ISBN:
978-1-911276-90-6

PUBLISHED BY:
Mortons Media Group Ltd,
Media Centre, Morton Way,
Horncastle,
Lincolnshire,
LN9 6JR.
Tel: 01507 529529

PRINTED BY:
William Gibbons and Sons,
Wolverhampton

COPYRIGHT:
©2019 Mortons Media Group Ltd.
All rights reserved.

MORTONS
MEDIA GROUP LTD

STEAM LEGENDS

That helped shape the modern world

A3 Pacific No. 60103 *Flying Scotsman* and B1 4-6-0 No. 61306 *Mayflower* climbing to Slochd Summit, between Aviemore and Inverness, on the Highland Main Line, with Steam Dreams' 'The Highlands and Islands' tour on May 10, 2019. TREVOR GREGG

One of the primary fruits of the Industrial Revolution, it is a gross understatement to say railways have shaped the modern world.

Journeys that at one time would have taken a week or more could be undertaken within a day, or even hours, thanks to the development of steam locomotive technology.

Every advance in locomotive technology was met with awe and wonder by the public, for whom the horse and cart had long been 'state-of-the-art' public transport.

The concept was invented and developed in Britain, where the early steam railways were little local affairs and often private industrial lines.

However, the opening of the world's first inter-city line – the Liverpool & Manchester Railway – heralded through the success of Stephenson's *Rocket* in the Rainhill Trials of 1829, sparked a flurry of trunk railway building, and brought the concept to a far wider and immediately receptive audience.

News of every major advance in railway science generated newspaper headlines, and ignited public enthusiasm.

Every ground-breaking or record-breaking feat by a new-type locomotive would see the footplate crew, designer and the machine itself feted as heroes, long before we entered the modern age of celebrity culture.

Names such as *City of Truro*, *Mallard* and arguably the most famous of them all, *Flying Scotsman*, became household names, and provided a source of ready inspiration to countless generations, not least of all to short-trousered schoolboy trainspotters, eagerly noting the number of every locomotive that passed by in their pocket money-priced Ian Allan locospotters' guides.

Advances in transport technology saw diesel and electric traction eventually replace steam haulage. British Railways ran its last main line steam train – the 'Fifteen Guinea Special' – on August 11, 1968, by which time many of those young lineside enthusiasts had packed up and gone home, never to return.

Yet there were others who didn't, and they formed the backbone of the railway preservation or heritage sector, which today is a sizeable slice of the UK's tourist economy.

And those who thought that interest in the past glories of steam would simply die and fade away were to be proved wrong – badly so, as it transpired.

Judging by soaring passenger numbers at heritage railways, interest in

Six decades after a member of the celebrated steam 'monsters' ran in revenue-earning service, Union Pacific Railroad Big Boy 4-8-8-4 No. 4014 enters Ogden Union station in Utah for the company's May 9, 2019 celebration to mark the 150th anniversary of the 'golden spike' completion of the First Transcontinental Railroad, linking the east and west coasts of the United States.

steam today often appears as great as in the days of old.

In spring 2019, two incidents served as stark reminders of the fact that steam legends have never died, and probably never will.

Flying Scotsman, which past surveys have indicated is the world's most famous steam locomotive, drew bumper crowds to the Swanage Railway in March, during very mixed weather, well out of season. And on May 5, British Transport Police issued stern warnings after trespassers at Elford, near Tamworth, were caught on camera stupidly standing a step away from the live running line in their attempt to capture No. 60103 on film as it hauled a leg of the Railway Touring Company's

'Great Britain XII' tour. Days before, concern had been expressed after a drone had been used to follow the A3 through Surrey, and amid plans to fit video cameras to the locomotive to record future lineside incursions, there was even talk among the rail authorities of banning *Flying Scotsman* from the national network for safety reasons if the problem persisted.

Meanwhile, across the Atlantic, steam fever was whipped up en masse by a sight that enthusiasts could only ever dream about, and which few ever dared hope to see: one of the eight surviving Union Pacific Railroad Big Boy behemoths being returned to steam to run a series of railtours.

Union Pacific undertook the

unbelievably complex overhaul in order to mark the 150th anniversary of the completion of the First Transcontinental Railroad in 1869, a seminal moment in US, and therefore world history.

Legends might die, but by their nature, they are never forgotten, and there are those in the heritage sector who have worked 'Mission Impossibles' to re-create long-extinct locomotives from the past.

The A1 Steam Locomotive Trust's Peppercorn 4-6-2 No. 60163 *Tornado* has enjoyed celebrity stardom along the lines of that afforded to *Flying Scotsman*, and in April 2019, we saw the emergence of a new Great Western Railway Saint? Its name, more than appropriately, is *Lady of Legend*!

Chapter 1

Puffing Billy – the world's oldest surviving steam railway locomotive – in the Science Museum in London. ROBIN JONES

Puffing like
BILLY-O!

It is not often the name of a railway locomotive becomes adopted as an everyday saying in the English language, but many believe that happened in the case of the world's oldest surviving steam locomotive.

IT IS generally accepted the world's first steam railway locomotive was built by Cornish mining engineer Richard Trevithick at Coalbrookdale in 1802, but it was, as far as can be ascertained, never demonstrated in public, and it is believed few people ever saw it.

The oldest surviving steam railway locomotive in the world is *Puffing Billy*, which was built in 1813/14 for Christopher Blackett, owner of Wylam Colliery, near Newcastle-upon-Tyne.

In 1805 Blackett had held talks with Trevithick, who supplied him with

drawings of a steam locomotive. The locomotive, of which only very basic details survive, was built by foundry owner John Winfield and was running at Gateshead in May 1805. It was designed to be lighter than the locomotive demonstrated by Trevithick on the Penydarren Tramroad in 1804, and which broke the rails because of its weight.

Blackett's 5ft-gauge waggonway was made of wooden rails. Trials of the locomotive were carried out, but Blackett did not want the locomotive and its perceived difficulties. Instead, it was said to have been converted into a

blower for the foundry.

Blackett approached Trevithick again in 1808 having relaid his five-mile waggonway as an iron plateway, arguing that this time it might well stand the weight of one of his locomotives, but he said he was too busy to oblige

So Blackett instead asked his colliery superintendent William Hedley to build him a locomotive.

At first, the pair looked at converting the Wylam waggonway to a rack-and-pinion system, as designed by Middleton Colliery coal viewer and inventor John Blenkinsop.

Puffing Billy runs past George Stephenson's boyhood home alongside the Wylam waggonway, as painted by artist Rob Embleton. DURHAM JOINT CURRICULUM STUDY GROUP.

Blenkinsop had looked at Trevithick's locomotives and drew the conclusion their big problem was lack of adhesion. Trevithick's relied on their weight to stop them slipping, but in the process broke the rails. So make locomotives lighter? The problem then would be they could not haul as many wagons.

Blenkinsop invented a scheme whereby the locomotive would gain extra adhesion through a central cogwheel which would engage with a toothed third rail in the centre of the track. He therefore invented the world's first rack-and-pinion railway and took out a patent for the design, decades before any were built to ascend the Swiss Alps. Thousands of locals were amazed by the first locomotive as it ran light engine at 10mph during its trial run on the 4ft-gauge Middleton Railway, and then several of them jumped aboard the wagons for a ride. It was estimated Blenkinsop's locomotives could do the task of 50 horses.

His locomotive *Salamanca* was the world's first commercially successful steam locomotive on the first commercially successful steam railway, which led to the colliery's profits soaring within two years thanks to its 'modern' transport taking coals to market.

Blackett considered that converting his Wylam waggonway to a Blenkinsop rack-and-pinion system would be far too expensive, despite the rave reviews it was generating.

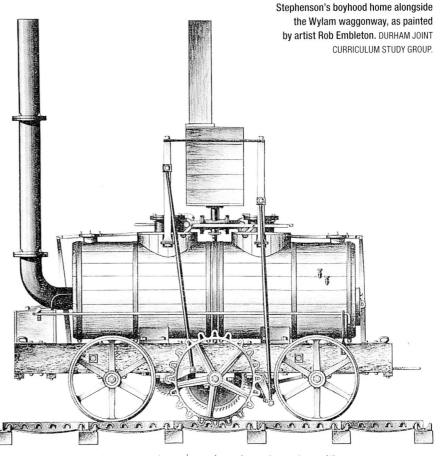

John Blenkinsop's rack-and-pion locomotive *Salamanca* of 1812. It impressed on the Middleton Colliery railway, but others remained unconvinced about the concept's superiority over adhesion-worked railways. In turn, William Hedley showed adhesion-worked lines were superior, as demonstrated by his *Puffing Billy* locomotive.

So Hedley went back to the Trevithick formula, to see if sufficient adhesion could be obtained using a smooth wheel on a smooth rail after all.

In 1813, he experimented with a carriage operated by four men, two each side standing on stages suspended from the frame. Each man turned a handle connected by a cross shaft to the one on the handle on the other side. A gear was set on the cross shaft, and in turn it engaged with a gear set on the wheel axle, thereby turning the wheels and moving the carriage along the plateway.

The carriage was loaded with various weights before more and more loaded coal wagons were attached until the wheels slipped. Hedley's experiment was a success: it proved that a sizeable train of loaded wagons could be hauled by the friction available from the driving wheels of a locomotive.

Hedley then upgraded the carriage into an experimental locomotive by adding a cast iron boiler, with one cylinder connected to a flywheel.

This 'travelling engine' as it was dubbed may have been nicknamed *Grasshopper*. Prone to stalling, and very much underpowered, it was not a success, but no matter – Hedley learned sufficient lessons in the process to design another locomotive, built by Wylam colliery's enginewright Jonathan Foster, with the aid of foreman blacksmith Timothy Hackworth.

The end result was markedly different to both Trevithick's and Blenkinsop's locomotives, and indeed, many others that would follow afterwards.

Puffing Billy incorporated a number of novel features, patented by Hedley, which were to prove important to the development of locomotives. It had two

Wylam Dilly in the Royal Museum in Edinburgh. TONY HISGETT*

vertical cylinders on either side of the boiler, and was partly enclosed by it. It drove a single crankshaft beneath the frames, from which gears drove and also coupled the wheels allowing better traction. A tender was attached to the chimney and firebox end to carry water and coal. Designed as a four-wheeler with flangeless wheels, it was converted to an eight-wheeler to share the load after the plate rails snapped. When the waggonway was relaid, it was converted back to four.

Hedley's locomotive became known as *Puffing Billy*, a name that also

entered the English language in phrases such as "puffing like Billy-o".

Another explanation is that the name derived from Joseph Billio, a hard-core Puritan 'hellfire and damnation' preacher at the United Reformed Church in Market Hill, Maldon, Essex, around 1696. Maldon townsfolk are convinced this that is the true origin, although the phrase did not enter common usage until long after Billio's death.

A success in its day, *Puffing Billy* regularly hauled trains of 50 tons between 4-5mph for nearly half a century, during which time it was repeatedly modified. It retired in 1862 and was eventually loaned by then colliery owner Edward Blackett to the Science Museum, which subsequently bought it off him for £200, where it is now on permanent display.

Wylam Dilly and *Lady Mary* were two similar locomotives built to improved *Puffing Billy* designs.

Puffing Billy and *Wylam Dilly* were both rebuilt in 1815 with 10 wheels, but were returned to their original condition in 1830 when the railway was again relaid with stronger rails.

'Dilly' was the name given to steam locomotives at Wylam Colliery. *Wylam Dilly* is preserved at the Royal Museum in Edinburgh.

The Wylam Waggonway ran past the front door of a cottage in Wylam village. It was there, in 1781, that George Stephenson was born. As an infant, he would have daily views of the trains passing close by, and one day he would invent a locomotive that would change the world. Adhesion-worked railways

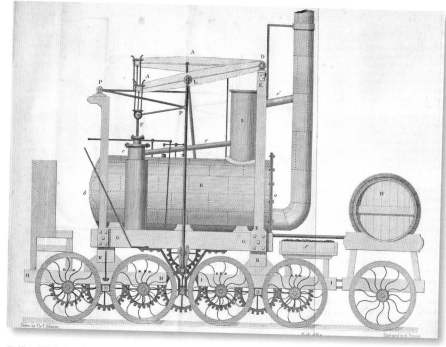

Puffing Billy in its eight-coupled form in 1813.

were clearly the way forward.

By the mid-1830s, Blenkinsop's rack systems had ceased operation, as they had by then long since been superseded by them.

It was not only George Stephenson who was influenced by *Puffing Billy*. In 1952 British light music composer Edward White wrote a melody named after the locomotive. It became the theme tune to the BBC Light Programme's Children's Favourites from 1952-66.

PUFFING BILLY – SECOND TIME AROUND.

Beamish Museum, in County Durham, has long been recognised as both the world leader in the study of early steam railways and the building of period replicas. That is both apt and ironic, because Durham is considered by historians to be the cradle of the steam railway, if not its birthplace.

In 1975, Beamish staff built a working replica of *Locomotion No. 1*, the first locomotive to run on the Stockton & Darlington Railway, the world's first public steam railway, on September 27, 1825.

While several locomotives from the embryonic age of steam survive, to return them to running order would be all but unthinkable. The sheer amount of original material which would need to be discarded and replaced – don't even mention the need for upgrading the design to modern safety methods – would severely damage their value as artefacts. So if you want to see them run again, build a replica!

In 2002, one of the most remarkable and distinctive of all new-build early locomotives was unveiled by Beamish Museum. The colossal *Steam Elephant* was an early locomotive that the world had all but completely forgotten.

All that had survived as evidence of the existence of this oversized and

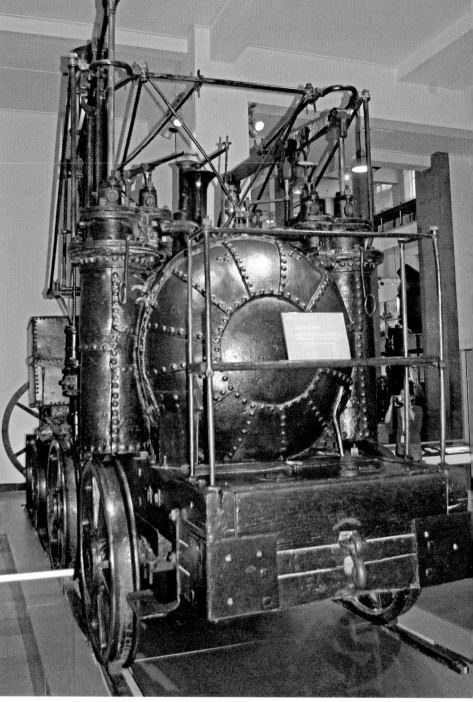

Puffing Billy in the Science Museum in South Kensington, as seen from the front. ROBIN JONES

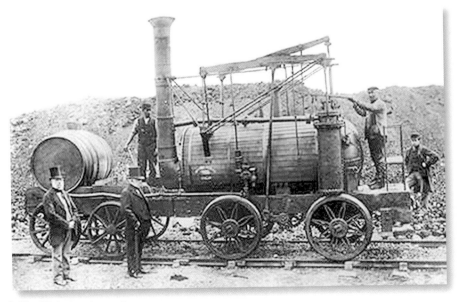

Puffing Billy's sister locomotive *Wylam Dilly* at work in 1862. BEAMISH MUSEUM

unwieldy beast of 1815 – very much a local and unique design by John Buddle and William Chapman for Tyneside's Wallsend Colliery – was a contemporary painting and a handful of basic sketches.

Yet from a mere handful of such evidence, combined with exhaustive technical research, Beamish Museum staff produced a new set of engineering drawings and set to work on replicating this mammoth of the dawn of steam.

The *Steam Elephant* now also runs on the museum's Pockerley Waggonway.

Next on the Beamish 'to do' replica list was none other than *Puffing Billy*.

Construction of a $400,000 *Puffing Billy* replica began in 2002, partially financed by the Hedley Foundation, a charity originally established by the descendants of William Hedley.

The 21st-century version was built to drawings produced by Dave Potter, with the boiler designed by Graham Morris, owner of Leighton Buzzard Railway-based Kerr, Stuart 0-4-0ST *Peter Pan*, with the project jointly overseen by Beamish's Jim Rees.

The locomotive, assembled by builder Alan Keef of Ross-on-Wye, Herefordshire, arrived at the museum in April 2006 and was immediately put through it paces.

The 'second' *Puffing Billy* also double-headed with the *Steam Elephant* replica over the Pockerley Waggonway. Shakedown trials, crew training and final testing by HM Railway Inspectorate followed, with *Puffing Billy* the second officially launched in July that year.

More fame was yet to come for this replica of an early steam legend.

In Whitsun 2007, the *Puffing Billy* replica was the star guest at the Dutch Museum Buurtspoorweg's 40th anniversary celebration.

The visit to The Netherlands was a welcome opportunity for the Beamish staff to assess the abilities of the Hedley-designed locomotive over longer distances, in this case over the five-mile line from Haaksbergen to Boekelo.

From a historical point of view, the visit of the 1813-designed locomotive could be seen as a curiosity, as the first train in The Netherlands ran only in 1839, between Amsterdam and Haarlem.

Nevertheless it was a superb opportunity for the Dutch public to see in action one of the engines that marked the very beginning of locomotive engineering.

Beamish Museum's working replicas of *Locomotion No.1* (left) and *Puffing Billy* as seen in 2008. BEAMISH MUSEUM

The *Steam Elephant replica* (left) and that of *Puffing Billy* on the Pockerley Waggonway at Beamish Museum. The waggonway opened in 2001, and represents the year 1825, the year the Stockton & Darlington Railway opened, the world's first public steam-operated passenger line. The engine shed is of a decidedly contemporary design. BEAMISH MUSEUM

In April 2017's Great North Festival of Transport, the *Puffing Billy* replica ran on the colliery line at Beamish Museum, coupled to a rake of chaldron wagons for the first time.
PAUL JARMAN/BEAMISH MUSEUM

Beamish Museum's £400,000 replica of *Puffing Bully,* newly arrived on April 27, 2006. BEAMISH

Chapter 2

The *Rocket*
FLEET

How much further can a locomotive go in terms of acquiring 'legendary' status than having a succession of full-size replicas built? Such is the worldwide fame of one of the most instantly recognisable steam locomotives of all – Stephenson's *Rocket*.

Stephenson's *Rocket* needs scant introduction. It was to all intents and purposes a trophy machine, built primarily to win a competition, the Rainhill Trials of October 1829, which was held not only to find a locomotive capable of hauling regular trains on the world's first inter-city line, the Liverpool & Manchester Railway, but to answer the question once and for all as to whether steam traction was the future of rail transport, as opposed to horse power or cable traction.

It had been a quarter of a century since Cornish mining engineer Richard Trevithick had given the first public demonstration of a steam railway locomotive, on the Penydarren Tramroad, near Merthyr Tydfil. However, while there were those who noted his invention, there were few prepared to take up the challenge commercially, and it was only during the time of the Napoleonic Wars, which provoked an acute shortage of supplies of horses and their feed, that northern colliery owners, anxious to ship their products to market, took a second look. As it was, Trevithick made no money from his world-shaping invention and indeed died in poverty.

While George Stephenson is popularly credited with building *Rocket*, it was his son Robert who took charge of its design and construction at the family firm of Robert Stephenson & Co in Newcastle-upon-Tyne, while in regular communication with George, and he may have been responsible for a lion's share of the project.

Huge crowds attended the trials, which began on October 6 – a grandstand was erected to accommodate them – and ultimately, *Rocket* was the outright winner from a total of five entrants.

Not only did the 0-2-2 win the £500 prize, it was immediately recognised as the most advanced steam locomotive of its day. On the last day of the trials, it hauled a carriage, conveying 25 passengers up an incline at 20mph.

By then no means the world's first successful steam locomotive, its revolutionary features included a multi-tubular boiler with a firebox separate from the boiler and built to double thickness, with 25 copper pipes taking the heated water into the boiler. These innovations provided the blueprint for future steam locomotive development worldwide.

Accordingly, *Rocket* received star billing at the opening of the Liverpool & Manchester Railway on September

The cut-away full-size replica of Stephenson's *Rocket* in the Great Hall of the National Railway Museum at York was built in 1935. It has been said if the replica was not in sections it could be made capable of steaming.

15, 1830, where the chief guest was the Tory Prime Minister, Arthur Wellesley, the first Duke of Wellington. Three special carriages had been built for the occasion, the finest of all for the Duke, whose train was hauled by Rocket-style 0-2-2 *Northumbrian*.

The official opening trains stopped at Parkside station, 17 miles from Liverpool, the halfway point of the line, so the locomotives could take on water, with passengers being told to stay on board. Sadly, Liverpool MP William Huskisson, who had earlier fallen out with the Duke and resigned from his cabinet, wanted to renew their friendship and alighted from his train to walk over to the Duke's plush carriage. The two men shook hands, and Huskisson was so elated he did not see *Rocket* approaching on the parallel track. Driver Joseph Locke could not slam on *Rocket's* brakes – because it did not have any.

Realising the danger too late, Huskisson pressed himself against the side of the carriage, and grabbed a door handle, but the door swung open. *Rocket* collided with the door, Huskisson fell on to the tracks in front of the oncoming train and sustained fatal leg injuries, dying later that night. It was not the world's first railway fatality as is so often erroneously reported, but the first to be given widespread publicity. Needless to say, it left a black cloud over what should have been a triumphant day on what was a seminal moment in world history.

History soon overtook *Rocket*, the innovations of which quickly led to the development of more advanced locomotives. In 1834, it was modified as a testbed for unsuccessful experiments, its cylinders and driving rods removed, with two of the engines installed directly

on its driving axle with a feedwater pump in between. The experiment proved to be a failure, but *Rocket* had already set out on a course that would completely change its appearance from that of the popular image in which it has been immortalised.

In 1836, *Rocket* was taken out of storage and restored, and sold to the Earl of Carlisle's Brampton Railway, a mineral railway on the borders of Cumberland and Northumberland that served eight collieries and had recently converted to standard gauge. It was sold again in 1838 to J Thompson, a nearby colliery owner.

Rocket was withdrawn by 1840, and returned to the Forth Street works in Newcastle, where it was built. It was hoped to have it displayed at the Great Exhibition at the Crystal Palace in 1851, but that never happened.

In 1862, it was given to the Patent Office Museum in London by the Thompson family. The Patent Office Museum became the Science Museum in 1909.

By then, *Rocket* was very different in appearance to the Rainhill Trials winner, having been repaired, modified or adapted over the years, but the legend would never die.

A contemporary illustration of *Rocket* in 1829, the year it won the Rainhill Trials.

Rocket in its bright yellow livery became the defining symbol of a watershed moment in history in which railways developed the power to shrink the world, eclipsing all steam locomotives that had preceded it.

While the surviving locomotive, now relegated to being a permanent static museum exhibit, bore scant resemblance to its once-proud former self which ran on the Liverpool & Manchester, there were those who saw mileage in parading it to an enthusiastic and admiring public again – if only as a replica. Indeed, *Rocket* has attracted more attention from replica makers than any other locomotive, and over a far longer time span.

The London & North Western Railway's chief mechanical engineer Francis William Webb built what would be the first of several full-size replicas at Crewe in 1881, for the centenary of George Stephenson's birth that year. The LNWR was a successor to the Liverpool & Manchester, having been formed by the Grand Junction Railway, the London & Birmingham Railway and the Manchester & Birmingham Railway in 1846, and so it could legitimately use *Rocket's* historical fame to reinforce its position at the Premier Line.

It was recorded that the replica *Rocket* was displayed at the International Exhibition of Navigation, Commerce and Industry in Liverpool, which was opened by Queen Victoria on May 11, 1886. Liverpool was hailed as the British Empire's principal port at the time, and the colossal, lavish expense of the event included an African village, 50 natives of India and Ceylon (now Sri Lanka), and camel and elephant rides.

LNWR publicity material continued to feature images of the replica for

STEPHENSON'S "ROCKET." Built 1829.

An official LNWR postcard depicting its replica of *Rocket*, believed to be the first of several. The LNWR made much publicity out of its *Rocket* heritage, having absorbed the Liverpool & Manchester Railway, for which it was built. ROBIN JONES COLLECTION

several decades. It was rebuilt in 1911, and was again exhibited in Liverpool in 1930 during celebrations to mark the centenary of the Liverpool & Manchester Railway. The replica was displayed on a raised platform outside the Museum of British Transport in Clapham, London from 1963 for a decade, after which it was scrapped, the wooden parts having rotted away.

A second replica was built, at

Rocket as depicted in a 1970s beermat by brewer Mackeson's. ROBIN JONES COLLECTION

Mount Clare in Maryland, USA, for the Columbian World's Exposition in 1893, and it was displayed again at the Baltimore & Ohio Railroad's Fair of the Iron Horse in 1927. Nothing more was heard of it afterwards.

What was either a working replica or a convincing movie prop was built in 1923 for the Buster Keaton silent movie *Our Hospitality* – a film based in the Wild West. It was very much a 'broad brush stroke' copy, and has the name *Rocket* painted on its side.

This replica appeared in the Al St John film The Iron Mule two years later, directed by Keaton's mentor, Roscoe 'Fatty' Arbuckle.

The fate of this replica is also lost in the mists of time: it may well have been discarded as a spent prop after the second movie was made.

Robert Stephenson & Hawthorns supplied and exported a replica *Rocket* to motor car magnate Henry Ford in 1929.

Unlike the version that appeared in the earlier Hollywood movies, Ford demanded it should be built to exacting standards.

He used it on his private track within his Greenfield Village museum in Dearborn, Michigan. That museum is

Model manufacturer Hornby inherited an OO-gauge Stephenson's *Rocket* set from the Tri-ang Railways catalogue in the 1960s, and later went on to produce a 3½in-gauge steam-operated model set, which now sells to collectors for around £300 second-hand. HATTONS

A Robert Stephenson & Hawthorns *Rocket* replica alongside *Flying Scotsman* sister LNER A1 Pacific No. 2578 *Bayardo*, which was built by the North British Locomotive Company in October 1924, rebuilt into an A3 in May 1928, and withdrawn and scrapped in 1961.

Was it a working replica or a convincing prop? Nobody knows for sure the fate of this *Rocket*-lookalike replica built for the 1923 Buster Keaton Wild West silent movie Our Hospitality.

now the Henry Ford Museum, and the replica took pride of place in the hall of fame, highlighting the great landmarks of the Industrial Revolution. It last steamed in 1949.

Three more replicas to the same plan and detail were built by none other than Robert Stephenson & Co in the Thirties. Indeed, it has been speculated one of these, and not the LNWR replica, was the one displayed at Liverpool in 1930.

One of the three was built for the Chicago Museum of Science and Industry, and the other two, sectioned to show the inner workings, were constructed for the Museum of the Peaceful Arts in New York – what became the New York Museum of Science and Industry – later being moved into the Rockefeller Center, and Britain's own Science Museum.

The latter static replica, constructed in 1935 and displayed alongside the original in the Science Museum, now stands in the Great Hall at the National

The *Rocket* replica built in 1929 for motor car manufacturer Henry Ford for his private museum in the USA. ENUII/VULCAN FOUNDRY

The cutaway cylinder of the 1935 *Rocket* replica. ROBIN JONES

LEFT: The 1935 static replica of *Rocket* coupled to a facsimile Liverpool & Manchester Railway coach inside the National Railway Museum. ROBIN JONES

The *Rocket* replica at the Museum of Science and Industry in Chicago. Non-working, it has rotating driving wheels.

Railway Museum, along with a pair of replica Liverpool & Manchester carriages, and is one of the venue's most popular exhibits.

By contrast, the current whereabouts of the New York replica remain unclear. It seems to have found new owners: a locomotive listed in a classic car auction catalogue as a sectioned replica of *Rocket* reportedly sold for $42,000 in 2004, and there is speculation it may now be in private hands in southern California, possibly Los Angeles.

Rumours have occasionally surfaced that it is being restored to steamable condition!

LEFT: Pocket-money-priced plastic kit maker Airfix produced an OO-gauge self-assembly model of *Rocket* which, first introduced by Kitmaster, proved enormously popular among youngsters for more than half a century. FREE PHOTO FUN

Scenes from Buster Keaton's 1925 silent movie Iron Mule, which again used what appeared to be a working locomotive replica of *Rocket* to comic effect. It has been suggested it was little more than a move prop that was discarded afterwards.

TODAY'S WORKING *ROCKET* – BUILT TWICE OVER!

A magnificent working replica of *Rocket* was built in 1979 by engineer Mike Satow and his Locomotion Enterprises for the Rocket 150 anniversary celebrations at Rainhill. This replica used some of the parts from the scrapped LNWR replica of 1881. Mike salvaged the metal components from the Clapham exhibit, including the frames (with modifications), trailing and tender wheelsets, upper chimney and sundry other bits and pieces. First of all, however, it was displayed in Kensington Gardens, London.

A frequent and popular visitor to heritage railways, it was fitted with a chimney shorter than the original in order to the clear the bridge at Rainhill, as there is now less headroom than when the line was built in the 1820s. It is now based at the National Railway Museum, and frequently visits heritage lines around the country.

In 2002, it featured in a 'replay' of the Rainhill Trials staged at the Llangollen Railway for the BBC TV programme Timewatch – Rocket and its Rivals – using modern-day replicas of the original contestants. Even though the locomotives were not the same, the winner was *Rocket*!

The 1979 *Rocket* also has the unique claim to having been built new twice.

In 2009 it was dismantled for overhaul and completely rebuilt by Victorian locomotive restoration experts at chartered surveyor and heritage steam engineer Bill Parker's Flour Mill Colliery workshops at Bream in the Forest of Dean, not only with a new boiler, but also new frames, the single component which gives a locomotive its identity. It returned to steam the following February.

The modern-day working replica of *Rocket* being rebuilt for the second time. Originally constructed in 1979, in 2010 it was taken to the Flour Mill workshop at Bream in the Forest of Dean, a market leader in the restoration of Victorian locomotives, to be overhauled. The plan was to replace the boiler. However, it was discovered the replica's frames were significantly out of size from the original design, so in the interests of accuracy it decided to start again with new frames, and then design the new boiler to fit the correct frames. As a result, the only components that still fitted were the front wheels and the cylinders, but all the fixings had to be new, because the diameter of the boiler to which they are all attached is different. Even the back wheels had to be replaced because they were the wrong diameter. Convention holds that the frames are the single component which gives an identity to a locomotive, and as they were replaced, the end product, which subsequently underwent running-in trials on the Avon Valley Railway, is in theory a new locomotive! BILL PARKER

LEFT: The 'new' *Rocket* replica hauls a Liverpool & Manchester Railway carriage along the Great Central Railway to Loughborough during a Golden Oldies gala on May 31, 2010. ROBIN JONES

Rocket on display in the Science and Industry Museum in Manchester in late-September 2018. Preserved in its latter-day form as an industrial locomotive, it bears little resemblance to the replicas of *Rocket* in its original form, with yellow-liveried cladding and wheels. NRM

BACK TO THE NORTH

Over the decades, *Rocket* has formed the basis of countless models, toys and ornaments.

In the Thomas & Friends television series, it was portrayed as *Stephen*, a friend of Sir Robert Norramby, Earl of Sodor. The name *Stephen* comes from its designer, Stephenson.

So the *Rocket* legend persists and with the passage of time continues to grow even bigger in stature, a permanent reminder of the time when Britain led the world in technology.

Having been displayed in the Science Museum since 1862, *Rocket* was loaned to Tyneside's Discovery Museum between June 22 and September 9, 2018, as a key exhibit in the landmark Great Exhibition of the North.

During the 80 days *Rocket* was on display, it was seen by more than 176,000 visitors. Discovery Museum and archives manager Carolyn Ball said: "It's been hugely popular and one of the star attractions."

On September 20, it was removed and taken by lorry to the Museum of Science & Industry in Manchester – which incorporates Liverpool Road station, the eastern terminus of the Liverpool & Manchester Railway into which *Rocket* would have regularly ran shortly after the line opened. It remained on display until late-April 2019 – afterwards

becoming a permanent exhibit in the National Railway Museum in York, where both its working and cutaway replicas are already based.

LOOKING INSIDE A LEGEND!

In 2018, the Science Museum Group published a high-resolution 3D model of *Rocket*, enabling audiences across the globe to examine it in unprecedented detail. Working with Science Museum Group colleagues, a team from ScanLAB spent 11 hours recording every angle of the original to create the 3D model using more than 200kg of camera, lighting and scanning equipment.

Scanning and photography was particularly challenging due to *Rocket's* colour, glossy texture and complex shape.

It was created using 22 high-resolution LIDAR scans and more than 2500 detailed photographs. After six weeks of processing the LIDAR data and 220 gigabytes of photography, a highly detailed point cloud was produced, containing spatial coordinates, colour and intensity values for a staggering 750 million points.

A further two weeks of processing was needed to produce several 3D models of *Rocket*, one of which – featuring 84,000 vertices – was published as *Rocket* went on display at the Science & Industry Museum

in Manchester (see above). *Rocket's* legendary efficiency and performance innovations, all of which are highlighted on the 3D model, include the multi-tubular boiler design and blastpipe, the use of a single pair of driving wheels, with a small carrying axle behind, and cylinders closer to the horizontal, all of which helped make the locomotive the fastest locomotive of its time.

Its ground-breaking design became the basis for subsequent steam locomotive development over the next 150 years.

The 3D model of *Rocket* has been published on the Science Museum Group Collection website at https://tinyurl.com/y5863pbn. Audiences can move the 3.3-ton locomotive around with ease on screen, inspect underneath and explore the innovations.

The model can also be downloaded from Sketchfab (sketchfab.com/models) under a Creative Commons non-commercial licence, enabling users to 3D print their own model of *Rocket*.

Measuring more than 13ft in length, *Rocket* is the most complex and largest item from the Science Museum Group Collection to be scanned.

George and Robert Stephenson changed the world with their prize-winning locomotive – but would never have imagined that one day they would be able to look at it from this viewpoint! Super detailed 3D images of *Rocket,* now freely available on the internet. SCIENCE MUSEUM

The replica of the *Stourbridge Lion*, built by the Delaware & Hudson Railroad for the 1939 New York World's Fair.

The United States is renowned as a world leader in technology, and sent the first manned space missions to the moon half a century ago. Yet the first steam railway locomotive to run in the US was built in Britain – at a foundry in the West Midlands.

The Stourbridge Lion:
THE FIRST ROAR OF STEAM... STATESIDE

Britain invented the self-propelled railway locomotive, believed to have been first built by Cornish mining engineer Richard Trevithick at Coalbrookdale in 1802 and successfully publicly demonstrated by him on the Penydarren Tramroad in South Wales two years later.

At the time, railways were horse-drawn affairs, the purpose of which was to link collieries and foundries to the nearest waterway or harbour. At first, Trevithick's inventions were considered more of a novelty than a series form of everyday transport, but in the next decade, many industrialists and their attendant engineers began to take a second look at his concept.

Horse-drawn tramways by then had been in use in Britain for two centuries or more, but it was only in the 1820s that the idea of railroads being used as an essential form of transportation in the United States attracted serious interest. By that time, several horse-drawn or incline railways were in the process of being built.

In 1823, the Delaware & Hudson Canal Company, which became the Delaware & Hudson Railway, was authorised to carry anthracite from the coalfields around Carbondale, Pennsylvania to New York City via a set of cable-operated incline railways powered by stationary steam engines.

The name of the locomotive took its name from the lion's face painted on the smokebox.

The company's original name came about because its first plan was to build a canal over the entire distance, but two years later, engineers began to consider railways, too.

John Bloomfield Jervis was appointed as the company's chief engineer in 1827, and drew up a scheme for a series of inclines linked by level railways over a distance of 17 miles. The company was impressed and gave him the go-ahead to build it, despite the fact rail technology had still not yet considered to have been wholly proven.

He sent his deputy engineer Horatio Allen to Britain on a railway fact-finding mission – and brought with him Jervis' specifications for locomotives that could be ordered for the Delaware & Hudson. Even though Allen was just 25, he was authorised to buy four locomotives if he felt they would be suitable.

In England, he met locomotive engineers Robert Stephenson and John Urpeth Rastrick of Foster, Rastrick & Company.

Rastrick had been there as near as might be possible to the dawn of the railway age. Born in 1780 at Morpeth in Northumberland, he completed an apprenticeship with his father, including work on steam engines. He worked first at the Ketley Ironworks in Shropshire and then formed a partnership with John Hazledine of Bridgnorth.

It was at Bridgnorth he built the world's first locomotive to haul fare-paying passengers – *Catch-me-who-can*, for Richard Trevithick. The locomotive and a carriage famously gave public rides on a trainset-style circle of track near the future site of Euston station in London.

In 1817, Rastrick left the partnership with Hazledine's company and moved to West Bromwich in the Black Country. June 1819 saw Rastrick and James Foster form Foster, Rastrick & Company at a site next to the Stourbridge Iron Works. There, a new foundry was constructed from 1820/21 to produce products for the partnership.

Allen wrote back to Jervis to let him know he had ordered four locomotives to be shipped to the Delaware & Hudson. There was one from Robert Stephenson & Company of Newcastle-upon-Tyne, the *Pride of Newcastle*, and three from Foster, Rastrick & Company, including the *Stourbridge Lion*.

While in England, Allen also ordered 290 tons of scrap iron from a foundry in Wolverhampton to help build the US line.

It was Stephenson's works which completed the first of the four locomotives, and it arrived in the USA nearly two months before the first from Foster, Rastrick, the *Stourbridge Lion*, which cost $2,914.90, was delivered to the States.

'Lion' was transported as a kit of parts from Liverpool aboard the ship *John Jay* and arrived back in New York on May 13.

It was then sent to the West Point Foundry, based in nearby Cold Spring, for reassembly and testing. US history

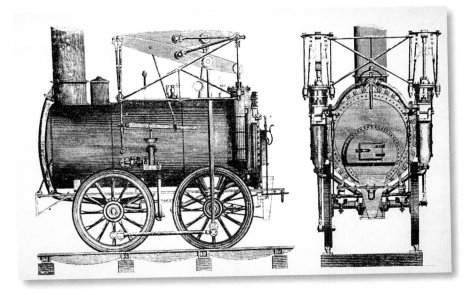

A lithograph of the *Stourbridge Lion,* the first railway locomotive to run in the United States, as built by Foster, Rastrick & Company.

was made when its trials began on August 5 and 'Lion' was shown to be in working order; it was also attracting thousands of sightseers who wanted to see it move.

August 8, 1829, saw 'Lion's' first official run along the completed length of line in Honesdale, Pennsylvania, with Allen in charge.

It was reported 'the fire was kindled and steam raised, and, under the management of Horatio Allen, the wonderful machine was found capable of moving, to the great joy of the crowd of excited spectators'.

Allen had no experience of driving a locomotive but he took the controls of the 'Lion', and invited spectators to ride with him. Wary of this strange beast, the like of which had never been seen running in America before, none of the crowd accepted the invitation.

Allen ran the *Stourbridge Lion* up and down the coal dock several times, pulled the throttle valve open, yelled farewell to the throng, and dashed away around a curve and over the raised trestle section

that crossed Lackawaxen Creek at 10mph.

He drove the 'Lion' for three miles along the track accompanied by the welcoming cheers of the crowd, the waving of flags and the booming of cannon, before reversing it back to its starting point.

Yes, the *Stourbridge Lion* was in roaring good form, but sadly the track was not up to scratch. Jervis had stipulated the engines should not weigh more than four tons, but 'Lion' weighed 7.5, and that proved its undoing.

'Lion' would never run along the track again. Soon, labourers began laying wooden planks between the rails so horses could pull wagons along it instead.

The two other Foster, Rastrick engines – Delaware and Hudson – arrived separately at New York in August and September 1829 before being shipped on to Rondout, and from there taken by canal to Honesdale.

As the canal company could not afford to buy iron rails, the *Stourbridge*

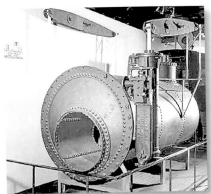

The boiler of the original *Stourbridge Lion* on public display at the Baltimore & Ohio Railroad Museum, Baltimore.

LEFT: A 1916 charcoal sketch by Clyde Osmer DeLand, depicting the *Stourbridge Lion* during its trial run on August 8, 1829. It was the first railway locomotive to run in the USA.

STOURBRIDGE LION'S HALF SISTER CLOSER TO HOME

A 'half sister' locomotive of the *Stourbridge Lion* was built by Foster, Rastrick, but this time for use in England.

In 1823, James Foster leased land at Shutt End, Kingswinford to exploit the mineral deposits there and built an ironworks. He wrote in 1825 to local landowner John William Ward, the 4th Viscount Dudley, proposing to build a railway to transport minerals from both their lands.

Accordingly, in 1827, an agreement to construct a standard-gauge railway between Shutt End colliery and a canal basin at Ashwood on the Staffordshire & Worcestershire Canal, was signed.

Agenoria had a much longer chimney than the *Stourbridge Lion*, with its name taken from the Roman goddess of industry.

It first ran when the line opened on June 2, 1829.

The opening day attracted crowds of spectators. *Agenoria's* first run saw it haul eight carriages filled with 360 passengers at 7.5mph. A second demonstration saw it pull 20 carriages, 12 filled with coal and eight with passengers, at 3.5mph.

For its final test of the day it ran for a mile with just the tender attached, carrying 20 passengers, reaching 11mph.

Agenoria ran in service on the line until the mid-1860s, with a replacement arriving in 1865.

Half forgotten and neglected, it was rediscovered on the colliery site, disassembled and covered with rubbish. One of its cylinders had been removed and used as a pumping engine.

It was reassembled and displayed at an exhibition in Wolverhampton in 1884, after which Foster gave it to the Science Museum in London.

Agenoria was loaned to the LNER's museum at York in 1937, and in 1951 was an exhibit at the Festival of Britain.

It returned to York in 1974 and is now displayed with a replica tender in the Great Hall of the National Railway Museum.

LEFT: Foster, Rastrick & Company's *Agenoria*, sister to the *Stourbridge Lion*, was a 'star' early locomotives exhibit in the Great Hall of the National Railway at York. It is the oldest complete locomotive in the museum. ROBIN JONES

Lion was housed in a shed after this impressive trail run and dismantled in 1834, so the boiler could be used in a local foundry in Carbondale. An attempt to sell all three Foster, Rastrick engines to the Pennsylvania Canal Commission proved fruitless, and the four locomotives ended up being used as a source of bar stock metal.

By that time, the railroad concept had become established in the US and the four were considered obsolete. US railroads were now building their own steam locomotives to far better suit their growing needs.

The first regular passenger railway in the USA to use steam locomotives was the Charleston & Hamburg, of South Carolina, which was authorised in 1827. On this line the first locomotive built for service, an engine called the 'Best Friend,' was running in December, 1830.

Yet a locomotive built in the West Midlands had made US history, and would never be forgotten – even though it never ran again.

Seeing steam was not to be used on the Delaware & Hudson, Allen moved to the South Carolina Canal & Railroad, where he became chief engineer in 1830.

The remains of the *Stourbridge Lion* passed into many hands over the ensuing decades.

In 1883, the Delaware & Hudson borrowed the boiler for display at the Exposition of Railway Appliances in Chicago. Sadly, a lack of security around the boiler's transportation allowed souvenir hunters, conscious of 'Lion's' history, to pull every loose item that they could off the now historic boiler, even resorting to hammers and chisels to remove parts of it.

What was left of the boiler was eventually acquired by the Smithsonian Institution in 1890, but the boiler had been badly damaged through years of use, neglect, and vandalism.

Some other components thought to have come from the *Stourbridge Lion* are also preserved, but experts conjecture they may have come from the sister engines.

The museum has made a few attempts to rebuild the locomotive with the parts that remain, but because other components are lacking, the locomotive's reconstruction has never been completed.

The Delaware & Hudson constructed its own replica of the *Lion* from

A US stamp depicting the *Stourbridge Lion*.

The Delaware & Hudson replica of the *Stourbridge Lion* at the Wayne County Historical Society.

A 1931 print of a painting of the *Stourbridge Lion* by Sheldon Pennoyer.

drawings, based on the parts remaining in existence, to run at the 1933 Century of Progress Exposition in Chicago.

The replica was relocated to Honesdale in 1941, and is now based at the Wayne County Historical Society Museum, which is located in a small brick building in Main Street, Honesdale, Pennsylvania, once a Delaware & Hudson Canal's Company office, and where the *Stourbridge Lion* started its maiden run.

A bid was made to steam it again in 2004, but the high cost of insurance was too high a deterrent, and also, the replica would need to be brought up to modern safety standards.

'Lion's' boiler is now on loan to the Baltimore & Ohio Railroad Museum in Baltimore.

Also, a replica built by the Delaware & Hudson, using the original 'Lion' blueprints, is based in Honesdale.

In October 2009, the US-based *Trains* magazine announced a project to build a full-size *Stourbridge Lion* replica had been launched.

A plaque commemorating the *Stourbridge Lion* at Honesdale, Pennsylvania. DOUG KERR*

Chapter 4

Looking both ways:
WHEN ROBERT FAIRLIE 'DOUBLED UP' STEAM

The Ffestiniog Railway is famous as the only place in the world where the legendary double Fairlie articulated 'back-to-back' steam locomotives can be seen in action. They were the product of a mid-Victorian inventor who sought to increase the versatility of steam locomotives, and for a time found a market for them in several countries overseas, too.

TOP: Double *Fairlie Merddin Emrys* at Harbour station, Porthmadog, where the Ffestiniog Railway joins the Welsh Highland Railway. The locomotive dates from 1879. JAMES WAITE/FF&WHR

From the outset, the railway concept has an inherited disadvantage over the road alternative. A horse and cart, and later a motor vehicle, can easily be turned so it is facing the right way. Not so easy for a classic steam locomotive. When it reaches the end of its route, it either has to be reversed via a turntable, or run backwards. Either way, a loop is needed for it to run round its train from one end to another.

They would have been an object of wonder when they were first introduced, and probably at first glance an object of ridicule, but inventor Robert Francis Fairlie's famous design showed what seemed in effect was two ordinary tank locomotives surgically stitched back to back.

It was in 1869 this revolutionary design first manifested itself on the Festiniog Railway in Snowdonia – and even though that line has long since spelt its name with two 'fs', (its name was changed in the heritage era to include both 'fs' in the name of the locality, an omission from the original Act of Parliament, which empowered it in 1832), they are still very much in evidence there today, as trademark locomotives of the line.

The Festiniog was originally a horse-drawn affair, laid to carry slate from the quarries at Blaenau Ffestiniog to the harbour at Porthmadog. However, in October 1863 steam locomotives were introduced, to allow longer slate trains to be run. This move also facilitated the official introduction of passenger trains in 1865, and in doing so it became the first narrow-gauge railway in Britain to carry passengers.

Fairlie was a business associate of George England, who supplied the first steam engines – 0-4-0 saddle tanks – to the Festiniog in 1863, from locomotive building company in New Cross, Surrey.

Fairlie trained in the railway workshops at Crewe and Swindon before becoming locomotive superintendent at the Londonderry & Coleraine Railway in 1852. Four years later he joined the Bombay, Baroda & Central India Railway, before returning to Britain.

His first double Fairlie was *The Progress*, an 0-4-4-0T built in 1865 by James Cross and Company of St Helens for the Neath & Brecon Railway. It proved a disappointment: having the draught from both halves of the boiler through one firebox was unsuccessful.

Cross built a second double Fairlie in 1866, *Mountaineer*, for the Anglesey

Central Railway. There followed a trio of 3ft 6in-gauge 0-6-6-0Ts for Queensland in Australia, but they were rejected as being overweight, and returned to England, regauged and re-sold.

Little Wonder, built by England in 1869 for the Festiniog, was a different matter, and brought its designer overnight fortune and fame.

England retired in 1869, and Robert Fairlie joined with England's son and J S Fraser to take over his works and to form the Fairlie Engine & Steam Carriage Co. England junior died within a few months, and the works were sold, with all locomotive production ceasing at the end of 1870. However, the Fairlie Engine & Rolling Stock Co continued as an office for design and for the licencing of Fairlie locomotive manufacture.

On February 11, 1870, Fairlie invited locomotive engineers from all over the globe to the Festiniog Railway to see *Little Wonder* in action, and railway companies from as far away Russia, Mexico, Turkey and Sweden were represented.

The event was a huge success, and left Fairlie with a bulging order book: not only that, but it did much to promote narrow-gauge steam, demonstrating it was a credible alternative to standard gauge in hill terrain. The Fairlie design meant the fireboxes and ashpans were not restricted by frame or track width, but only by the overall loading gauge.

By 1876, 43 different railways had operated his engines. However, the only railways where the type was truly successful in the long term was Mexico, New Zealand and the Festiniog. More than 50 Fairlies were supplied to Mexico over four decades, including 49 massive 0-6-0+0-6-0s, which remained in use until the 1920s.

The problems many of the buyers found were the limited capacity for fuel and water caused by the lack of a tender, the flexible steam pipes being prone to leakage and wasting of power, and the absence of unpowered wheels, which on 'normal' types of steam locomotive act as stabilisers. Early Fairlies had a tendency for rough riding and were more susceptible to derailments: *Little Wonder* was worn out and replaced by the Festiniog after less than two decades of intensive use.

Fairlie also produced 'single' versions, resembling 'normal' locomotives. Effectively, a double Fairlie cut in half, they had a single articulated power bogie combined with an unpowered bogie under the cab, maintaining the ability to negotiate sharp turns. Popular in the USA, a single Fairlie 0-4-4 tank ran on the Swindon Marlborough & Andover Railway and three 0-6-4T were bought by the North Wales Narrow Gauge Railways, predecessor of the Welsh Highland Railway.

Fairlie gave the Festiniog Railway Company a perpetual license to use the Fairlie locomotive patent without restriction in return for using the line to demonstrate *Little Wonder*, which became the first of six to be owned by the company.

George England died in 1878 and Fairlie on July 31, 1885.

The Ffestiniog is one of Europe's most spectacular heritage railways, weaving its way through Snowdonia's slate country, and one of its trademark features is the regular use of double Fairlies.

Indeed, in modern times, it has made the type its own.

The second double Fairlie to arrive was *James Spooner*, which became the line's No. 8. It was supplied by Avonside, and lasted in service until 1933 when it was scrapped, the fate which befell *Little Wonder* in 1882.

The line's third double Fairlie – No. 10 *Merddin Emrys*, named after the sixth century Welsh poet – was delivered in 1879, and is still in service today. It underwent a major rebuild in 1987/8 with new tanks.

No. 11 *Livingston Thompson* was built at the line's own Boston Lodge works in 1886. Now out of service, it has been restored for static display, and is a star exhibit in the Great Hall at the National Railway Museum in York.

The Festiniog Railway fell into disuse after the Second World War, but following the success of the Talyllyn Railway revival in 1951, which kick-started the volunteer-led-operation heritage railway movement, the Ffestiniog was next to be tackled by enthusiasts.

The moribund line was taken over by volunteers in 1954, under the leadership of businessman Alan Pegler, who in 1963 bought *Flying Scotsman* from British Railways. The revivalists began to reopen the railway in stages from Porthmadog Harbour station and finally reached Blaenau Ffestiniog on May 25, 1982, the 150th anniversary of Royal Assent to the Festiniog Railway Act of 1832. In reopening the 13½-mile line, the revivalists needed to build a deviation around the Central Electricity Generating Board's hydro-electric power Llyn Ystradau reservoir, which had flooded part of the original line.

The deviation included a spiral loop unique in Britain, and is considered one of the greatest achievements of the preservation era.

As the revived line grew longer, the preservationists needed more motive power for bigger trains. They turned to historic Boston Lodge Works to build their own – and chose a double Fairlie design!

The second double Fairlie – *Mountaineer* – was built in 1866 by James Cross of St Helens. It was operated for a short time on the Neath & Brecon Railway, but like the first ordered by the line, *The Progress*, proved unsuccessful.

The Festiniog Railway's first Fairlie, *Little Wonder*, at Porthmadog in the 1870s. It brought its designer fame and fortune with a bumper order book from impressed overseas buyers. FR CO ARCHIVES

THE SECOND EARL OF MERIONETH

The new double Fairlie would be the second locomotive to carry the name Earl of Merioneth. The first, originally named No. 3 *Livingston Thompson*, subsequently named *Taliesin*, was renamed *Earl of Merioneth* in 1961.

Furthermore, the project was a major landmark in the history of Britain's new-build locomotives, for the new double Fairlie was the first new full-size engine built for a full-size heritage railway.

It was built under the Fairlie patent, to which the Ffestiniog, as stated above, has a licence in perpetuity to use.

Some may argue new locomotives built previously for the 15in-gauge Ravenglass & Eskdale Railway should instead be regarded as the 'first'. However, these engines, like those on the Fairbourne, Cleethorpes Coast Light and Romney, Hythe & Dymchurch railways, are in so many respects 'halfway houses' between miniature railways and narrow gauge, and in effect are scaled-down replicas, based on main line types.

However, *Earl of Merioneth* is not a replica of any previous double Fairlie,

but one which was built to a modern updated design of the Victorian concept, with sloping square tanks.

Building work for the new double Fairlie – the third locomotive to be turned out from Boston Lodge – began in 1972 following delivery of the boiler. They were designed like the original Fairlies for coal burning, with oil tanks and oil burning equipment fitted in 1978 before the boiler was first steamed.

It incorporated the power bogies and some other parts from *Livingston Thompson*, while the superheated boiler was made by Hunslet of Leeds. New steel wheels were cast by British Rail Engineering at Crewe, and the axles and wheels were machined by JIP Engineering Ltd of Willenhall, Staffordshire, for assembly at Boston Lodge.

Carrying the name *Earl of Merioneth* in English on one side and *Iarll Meirionnydd* (in Welsh) on the other, it made its first trip out of the works and across the Cob on June 12, 1979.

On Saturday, June 23 that year, it was formally named by the railway's late general manager Allan Garraway at Porthmadog Harbour station, with older sister *Merddin Emrys* in attendance alongside, carrying an 1879-1979 headboard. Five days later, the new locomotive hauled a 12-coach test train to Tanygrisiau.

The new locomotive hauled its first passenger train on July 19, 1979, and was then rostered for two trips a day. It showed exactly what it could do on August 12, when following the failure of another locomotive, it hauled 12 trains up the line without any difficulty.

Double Fairlie No. 12 *David Lloyd George* dates from 1982 and is the most powerful of the type of the line. It is seen heading towards Penrhyn with a Porthmadog-bound train. ROGER DIMMICK/Ff&WHR

The new *Earl of Merioneth* was not to everyone's liking. Its angular appearance with rather utilitarian modern box-like side tanks led to it being nicknamed 'The Square'.

Accordingly, at its first 10-year overhaul in 1989, the opportunity was taken to attempt to soften its appearance by fitting brass dome covers and copper-capped chimneys, both of which were formerly fitted to *Merddin Emrys* prior to that locomotive's 1988 rebuild. The livery was also adjusted to include more traditional lining.

In 1992, *Earl of Merioneth* was found to have serious cracks around the boiler throatplate, reportedly because of a design-flaw in the two 1971-built Hunslet boilers.

At the same time, the railway was building a second new double Fairlie – No. 12 *David Lloyd George* – also at Boston Lodge, but to a far more conventional appearance. This particular project began at the same time as a proposal to build a new boiler for *Earl of Merioneth* – but got carried away with itself so much so that a new locomotive appeared. Indeed, it was decided to withdraw *Earl of Merioneth* and use its bogies and other components to complete the new locomotive.

David Lloyd George, grant-funded by a development programme known as the INcreased CApacity (or INCA) project, was designed to match the appearance of the 1880s Fairlies, but with many improvements to performance and range, including a completely new tapered boiler design with higher degree of superheat, *Earl of Merioneth* was then stored as a kit of parts until 1995/6, while repairs were made to the boiler.

However, the same problems were also being experienced with the boiler on *Merddin Emrys*, which resulted in it being withdrawn in 1996.

So as to keep two double Fairlies running, *Earl of Merioneth* reappeared in 1997 with bogies and burners from *Merddin Emrys*, and also new round smokeboxes, which further 'smoothed' its appearance.

Despite being built as an oil burner – the Ffestiniog started converting its engines to oil firing in the early-1970s in a bid to reduce lineside fires in the Snowdonia National Park – *Earl of Merioneth* was converted to coal firing in 2007, because of the by-then significant difference in the prices of oil and coal. As a coal burner, it re-entered traffic on May 27 that year.

In 2012, *Earl of Merioneth* hauled a special train to commemorate the 20th anniversary of the line reopening to Blaenau Ffestiniog.

Regarding *David Lloyd George*, because its boiler is designed to operate at a higher pressure and has a greater degree of superheat than any other double Fairlie example, it is the most

Earl of Merioneth approaching Penrhyn with a Porthmadog-bound train on August 24, 2009. The box-like 'modern' steam design of this 1979 new-build earned it the nickname of 'The Square', and it is now in store indefinitely. ROGER DIMMICK/Ff&WR

powerful steam locomotive to run in normal service on the Ffestiniog. It is able to haul 12 coaches efficiently and economically, and was designed from the outset to be oil fired. It was named after David Lloyd George, the Liberal party prime minister who grew up locally and travelled on the line.

On May 28, 2012, *David Lloyd George* headed a 'special' carrying the Olympic torch.

An appeal had been launched in 2010 to build two new bogies to fit beneath No. 12. Its bogies were removed in February 2013 and fitted to *Earl of Merioneth*, and the boiler was stripped, retubed and converted from oil firing to coal.

During the winter of 2013 and early-2014, the locomotive was reassembled with both of its bogies on their wheels and valve gear fitted, and new taller chimneys installed. No. 12 returned to service in May 2014.

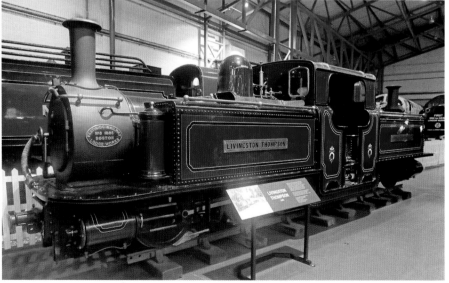

Built in 1886, *Livingston Thompson* was the Festiniog Railway's fourth double Fairlie. It is on permanent display in the National Railway Museum at York. ROBIN JONES

New-build single *Fairlie Taliesin* and *Merddin Emrys*, the oldest of the operational original double Fairlies on the Ffestiniog Railway, double-heading a Victorian train at Bron Madoc. CHRIS PARRY/FF&WHR

A SEVENTH DOUBLE FAIRLIE IN THE OFFING

In April 2016, the Ffestiniog Railway announced that *Earl of Merioneth* would be withdrawn and replaced by a new double Fairlie, to be named *James Spooner*.

Only its power bogies, built in 1986, were serviceable, and they are in need of heavy overhaul and new tyres. The decision was made by the railways' board that building a new locomotive was the best approach rather than patching up one that is effectively life-expired. The bogies and expensive fitting, such as pressure gauge, water gauges and injectors from the 1979 new build, were set to be removed for use on the new locomotive, with the rest of the body being left intact on its original bogies. That would allow for the 1979 locomotive to be restored in its own right in the future.

In December 2016 a fundraising appeal was announced for all new components for *James Spooner*.

Earl of Merioneth bowed out of service on Sunday, April 8, 2018. Its last train was a staff and volunteers' evening special, with proceeds from the ticket sales being donated to the local air ambulance service. Donations and the auction of the special headboard raised £3200.

Soon after its withdrawal, *Earl of Merioneth's* bogies were exchanged as planned. Since then the locomotive has been dry-stored at the back of the Boston Lodge heritage carriage shed.

A long-time favourite of the operating staff, there are various unofficial plans to return it to service using either its original boiler, the second of the two new double engine boilers, or using *Merddin Emrys's* boiler after it has finished its current 10-year ticket.

The new *James Spooner* will carry the number 8, as did its predecessor. It will have a traditional appearance, yet will be clearly identifiable alongside *Merddin Emrys* and *David Lloyd George*, with stovepipe chimneys and a removable cab roof centre section reminiscent of *Merddin Emrys*, as originally built. It is hoped some original components and design details will be incorporated into the new locomotive.

It is planned that the new *James Spooner* will enter traffic in 2020, in time for the 150th anniversary of the *Little Wonder* trials in 1870, when the world's first successful double engine hauled a train of 111 slate wagons, six carriages, 60 passengers and 12 goods wagons, 1350ft long.

The Festiniog also owned a single Fairlie, the 1876-built *Taliesin*, which was scrapped in 1935. A replica was built at Boston Lodge in 1999, using some parts from the original: there are those who would therefore like to consider it a 'rebuild' rather than a copy.

The boiler barrels for the new double Fairlie *James Spooner*, now being built in Boston Lodge Works. CHRIS PARRY/FF&WHR

Fairlies, including examples built in the UK by Avonside, Sharp, Stewart, and the Yorkshire Engine Company as 0-6-6-0Ts, were supplied to Russia, with further batches built in Germany. They entered service on a line between Tambov and Saratov, and on the Surami Pass of the Transcaucasus Railway, and were used until displaced by electrification in 1934.

WHAT OF THE FAIRLIES THAT SERVED ABROAD?

Josephine, a double Fairlie, is preserved in New Zealand's South Island at Dunedin, and a 60cm-gauge double Fairlie tramway-type engine that ran on a French narrow gauge line is at the Dresden Transport Museum in eastern Germany.

Until recently, it was thought there were no other double Fairlies or remains thereof surviving in Britain.

However, in June 2004, *Heritage Railway* magazine revealed two boilers from scrapped standard-gauge double Fairlies had been rediscovered in Burry Port, South Wales. The discovery was made by the Gwendreath Railway Society, which wants to reopen the Burry Port & Gwendreath Valley Railway, on which they ran.

It is believed one of the boilers belonged to an 0-4-4-0T, originally named *Pioneer*, but later renamed *Mountaineer*, and which in 1869 was only the second engine to be built by the Fairlie Steam & Carriage Company.

The other boiler is believed to come from 0-6-6-0T *Victoria*, one of the aforementioned early Fairlies returned from Queensland, and later sold to the Burry Port line. The boilers were scrapped around the turn of the century, and are now 6ft underground – in use as stormwater culverts!

The society has made the local authority aware of its interest in the boilers, which are said to be in reasonable condition, taking their use for the past century into account.

Undoubtedly, they are historically valuable artefacts, and will be retrieved if ever the chance presents itself. They could not be considered themselves as the basis for any new-build locomotive project, but could be used as a template to build a new boiler, or two.

To summarise, Fairlie's invention may seem weird by comparison with other steam locomotives today, but he was not far wide of the mark. Most main line diesels and traction units today have cabs at either end and turntables are a scarcity on the national network.

In hindsight, the double Fairlies, or at least the thinking behind their design, might therefore be seen as light years ahead of their time.

Apart from the Ffestiniog Fairlies, the sole-surviving locomotive of the type is *Josephine*, one of a pair built in 1872 by the Vulcan Foundry in England, and shipped as a kit of parts to New Zealand for use on the 3ft 6in-gauge Dunedin and Port Chalmers Railway – which had, yes you guessed, Robert Fairlie as its consulting engineer! The New Zealand Railways E class double Fairlie is now on static display in the Otago Settlers Museum, Dunedin. BENCHILL*

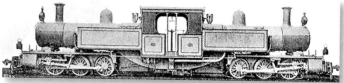

Vulcan Foundry built this double Fairlie for Burma Railways.

LEFT: The Ferrocarril Mexicano used 49 huge 0-6-6-0 Fairlies, imported from England, on a mountainous stretch of line between Mexico City and Veracruz. Very impressive in terms of power, they were used until the route was electrified in the 1920s.

Chapter 5

'Ton-up Truro': a reluctant legend?

In 1904, Great Western Railway icon No. 3440 *City of Truro* could have been hailed as the fastest locomotive in the world after being clocked at 102.3mph – yet the company waited 18 years to confirm the feat, because of public fears about speeding trains.

GWR 4-4-0 No. 3440 *City of Truro* acquired its immortality not for what it definitely achieved, but what it *probably* did – reportedly being the first steam locomotive in the world to reach and exceed the 100mph barrier.

It was recorded – unofficially, but apparently with a high likely degree of accuracy – as having attained 102.3mph while descending Wellington Bank in Somerset with the 'Ocean Mails Special' from Plymouth to Paddington on May 9, 1904.

By rights that feat should have bestowed the 2000th locomotive to be built with instant stardom. However, because of a prevailing mood of public opinion of the day against speeding trains, *City of Truro* was destined to become a reluctant legend, its status very much a slow burner.

Its feat was not acknowledged by the GWR until three years later, even though a report of the 100mph run appeared in two local newspapers the following day, after William Kennedy, a mail van worker on board, conducted some unofficial timings using his stopwatch.

City of Truro (later renumbered 3717) was an example of Chief Mechanical Engineer George Jackson Churchward's first design, the 20-strong 4-4-0 City of 3700 class, designed for hauling express passenger trains.

Ten of these locomotives were rebuilt from his predecessor William Dean's Atbara class, the first (No. 3405) being converted in September 1902 and the rest following between 1907-9. The new 10 were built at Swindon in 1903, with *City of Truro* being the eighth, outshopped from the works in April 1903. All 10 were named after cities on

time would correspond to a speed of 102.3mph.

Sadly, the driver spotted a gang of platelayers standing on the tracks a quarter of a mile away ahead, and braked fiercely while they moved aside, carrying on into Taunton at just 80mph, ruining the recorder's chance to confirm the speed.

Furthermore, there was no secondary timer on board to agree the claimed speed, so it was never taken as an official record.

Conscious of the need to preserve the GWR's reputation for safety, the company at first allowed only the overall timings for the run to be published, despite the contemporary report of 100mph in the Plymouth press mentioned above.

When Rous-Marten wrote an article that appeared in *The Railway Magazine* a month later, he merely described the trip as setting "the record of records".

He wrote: "It is not desirable at present to publish the actual maximum rate that was reached on this memorable occasion", and restricted his account to reporting that the train reached the minimum of 62mph logged on the ascent of Whiteball summit.

Rous-Marten first published the maximum speed in October 1905, but he did not name the locomotive or the railway company involved.

In the *Bulletin of the International Railway Congress*, he wrote: "On one occasion when special experimental tests were being made with an engine having 6ft 8in coupled wheels hauling a load of about 150 tons behind the tender down a gradient of 1-in-90, I personally recorded a rate of no less than 102.3 miles an hour for a single quarter-mile, which was covered in 8.8 seconds, exactly 100 miles an hour for half a mile, which occupied 18 seconds, 96.7 miles an hour for a whole mile run in 37.2 seconds; five successive quarter-miles were run respectively in 10 seconds, 9.8 seconds, 9.4 seconds, 9.2 seconds and 8.8 seconds.

"This I have reason to believe to be the highest railway speed ever authentically recorded. I need hardly add that the observations were made with the utmost possible care, and with the advantage of previous knowledge that the experiment was to be made, consequently without the disadvantage of unpreparedness that usually attaches itself to speed observations made in a merely casual way in an ordinary passenger train.

"The performance was certainly an

the GWR system and were originally numbered 3433-42.

At the time, the GWR was engaged in fierce competition with its great rival in the West Country, the London & South Western Railway, to see which could bring ocean mails from Plymouth to London the fastest, and while they had not been given permission to do so, some of the Paddington empire's drivers were determined to show what they and their Swindon-built engines could do.

On the day, it was the job of driver Moses Clements to take the train to Paddington, and by the time the train

– hauling a light load of eight-wheeled postal vans with around 1300 large bags of mail on board, total weight 148 tons – had reached the South Devon banks, it appeared he had decided to "go for it".

As the locomotive raced down the gradient from Whiteball Tunnel on the far side of Exeter, it was going faster than any member of the class had gone before.

On board the footplate was timer Charles Rous-Marten, who at around 10.45am recorded 8.8 seconds between two quarter-mile posts on the descent down Wellington Bank. If exact, this

City of Truro approaches Norchard (High Level) with a passenger service during a visit to the Dean Forest Railway on June 16, 2010. ROBIN JONES

epoch-making one. In a previous trial with another engine of the same class, a maximum of 95.6 miles an hour was reached."

It was only in the edition of *The Railway Magazine* in December 1907, nearly four years after the event, that the alleged speed of 102.3mph appeared publicly for the first time – and even then was not attributed to

a particular engine. However, Rous-Marten revealed the identity on the April 1908 edition, shortly before he died.

Yet it was not until 1922 that the GWR officially confirmed *City of Truro's* feat.

Then, the GWR published a letter written in June 1905 by Rous-Marten to James Inglis, the company's general manager, giving further details of the run.

Rous-Marten had written: "What happened was this: when we topped the Whiteball Summit, we were still doing 63 miles an hour; when we emerged from the Whiteball Tunnel we had reached 80; thenceforward our velocity rapidly and steadily increased, the quarter-mile times diminishing from 11 sec. at the tunnel entrance to 10.6 sec., 10.2 sec., 10 sec., 9.8 sec., 9.4 sec., 9.2 sec., and finally to 8.8 sec., this last being equivalent to a rate of 102.3 miles an hour.

"The two quickest quarters thus occupied exactly 18 sec. for the half-mile, equal to 100 miles an hour. At this time the travelling was so curiously smooth that, but for the sound, it was difficult to believe we were moving at all."

Doubts over the record have focused on the power of the locomotive and some contradictions in Rous-Marten's passing times. However, his milepost timings are consistent with a speed of 100mph or just over. This sequence of eight quarter-mile timings is thought to start at milepost 173, the first after the tunnel, with the maximum speed at milepost 171.

Modern-day research has examined the evidence and used computer simulation of the locomotive performance to prove a speed of 100mph was possible – and that Rous-Marten's timings indeed support such a speed.

City of Truro, with its original 1903 number and in late-Victorian (1881) GWR livery, in steam at Barrow Hill roundhouse in August 2008. HUGH LLEWELLYN*

City of Truro running at Didcot Railway Centre during the GWR 175 celebrations in 2010. TONY HISGETT*

SO WHY THE SECRECY?

In the early hours of Monday, July 13, 1896, the 8pm Down 'Highland Express' from Euston to Scotland hauled by LNWR locomotives No. 2159 *Shark* and No. 275 *Vulcan* derailed at the Dock Street points to the north of Preston station in the middle of the night.

Suddenly, the whole train was ploughing its way along the track, but the drivers kept their cool and brought the train to a standstill within a distance of 80 yards.

Both locomotives and the leading coaches were badly damaged, but the train was lightly loaded and only one of its 16 passengers, a young man called Donald Mavor, was killed.

A sharp curve at the north end of the station by the goods yard had a 10mph restriction.

It was later ascertained that the express had been travelling around 40-45mph through the station. When it hit the speed restricted curve, instead of going round it the train effectively carried on in a straight line. The engines ploughed through the goods yard, with the train coming to rest just short of a bridge wall.

Overnight, there mushroomed outright hostility to what was widely seen as placing life and limb at risk for the sake of breaking speed records in pursuit of railway company prestige.

Yes, there had been far worse accidents in terms of casualty figures, but this one was different, for it marked a watershed in public opinion towards trains running at such high speeds.

In the summers of 1888 and 1895, the nation had been gripped by reports of what railway historians now term the 'Races to the North'.

A contemporary sketch of the wreckage at Preston station after the early morning fatal crash on July 13, 1896. The crash provoked an overnight shift in public opinion against speeding trains, and was one of the reasons why the GWR kept quiet about *City of Truro's* feat on Wellington Bank for 18 years.

These occasions saw passenger trains from rival companies that would literally race each other to see which could reach Edinburgh from London in the quickest time over the two main trunk routes, the East and West Coast Main Lines. Driven by commercial rivalry, in 1888 the Great Northern Railway and the North Eastern Railway ran the East Coast service from King's Cross in competition against the London & North Western Railway and Caledonian Railway from Euston on the West Coast. The supposed 'races' were never official, and the companies publicly denied that what happened could in any way be described as racing.

By the 1890s an East Coast route had been established further north through Scotland over the Forth and Tay bridges, allowing the North British Railway to provide a reasonably direct Edinburgh to Aberdeen service.

Accordingly, it extended the East Coast consortium's King's Cross to Scotland route, as the NER had running rights to Edinburgh. However, the Caledonian already had a route connecting Carlisle and Aberdeen via Stirling and Perth.

So in 1895 a second 'race' broke out, but this time with the added excitement of arriving at the same station in Aberdeen. Indeed, after some 500 miles from London, the two routes converged to being in sight of each other just before Kinnaber Junction, from where there was a single track to Aberdeen. The press loved it.

However, the repercussions of the Preston accident sent shockwaves through the rail industry which would hamper progress for the next four decades.

City of Truro departs from Bristol Temple Meads with the 'Cornish Riviera Express' in March 2005.
HUGH LLEWELLYN*

City of Truro back at its birthplace, inside Swindon's STEAM – Museum of the Great Western Railway, which was set up inside part of the company's great works. Pictured on March 4, 2019, the locomotive is on loan from the National Railway Museum until 2021. CLIVE G

BELOW: *City of Truro*, repainted in the colours it carried in latter-day GWR service as No. 3717, at Didcot Railway Centre on May 1, 2010, the opening day of the venue's nine-day GWR 175 extravaganza.
FRANK DUMBLETON/GWS

City of Truro rounds the curve at Langstone Rock as it approaches Dawlish Warren, Isambard Kingdom Brunel's South Devon coastal route, while returning from Plymouth to Bristol Temple Meads with a Vintage Trains excursion on December 3, 2004. BRIAN SHARPE

TODDINGTON MODEL LAUNCH

A new finescale OO-gauge model *City of Truro* was launched in early December 2009 in a bid to raise tens of thousands of pounds for the National Railway Museum. The press launch was staged at Toddington on the Gloucestershire Warwickshire Railway, on December 4, where *City of Truro* is based, before which the company kept details of its latest release under wraps, although rumours of its appearance appeared on website discussion forums in the days beforehand. Graham Hubbard (right), managing director of Bachmann Europe plc, presented one of the first models to the railway's engineering director Andrew Goodman to mark the occasion. It was Andrew who had first mooted the idea of returning No. 3440 to steam nearly a decade before. After the presentation, the full-size version hauled a special train to Cheltenham Racecourse station (pictured) and back to mark the occasion. ROBIN JONES

Two National Collection legends side by side: No. 3440 *City of Truro* and LNER V2 2-6-2 No. 4771 *Green Arrow* on the Gloucestershire Warwickshire Railway on August 25, 2007. Both locomotives have now not steamed for several years, and at the time of writing there are no current plans to restore them to running order. TONY HISGETT*

WAS *CITY OF TRURO* THE FIRST?

However, it seemed that despite the public reaction in the aftermath of the Preston crash, trains would still be run at very high speeds, albeit for testing purposes, but nobody broadcast the fact.

'Truro's' exploit came nearly five years after a series of high-speed test runs on the Lancashire & Yorkshire Railway's Liverpool Exchange-Southport line using locomotives from John Aspinall's newly introduced 'High Flyer' 4-4-2 class.

Did New York Central & Hudson River Railroad 4-4-0 No. 999, pictured in Syracuse, reach 100mph 11 years before *City of Truro's* unofficial run on Wellington Bank? The claim has long been disputed. No. 999 was later preserved at the Museum of Science and Industry in Chicago.

The principal express engine of the L&Y, the class had the largest boilers fitted to any British engine, but their 7ft 3in-diameter driving wheels were rare for a coupled-wheel engine.

It was reported on July 15, 1899 one such train formed by No. 1392 and five coaches, and timed to leave Liverpool Exchange at 2.51pm, was recorded as passing milepost 17 in 12.75mins, by lineside enthusiasts.

While this gives a start-to-pass speed of 80mph, given the permanent 20mph restriction at Bank Hall and the 65mph restriction at Waterloo, it has been postulated this train attained 100mph.

Sadly, the railway company never published details or timings of this trip: it is only because passing times were unofficially noted by local enthusiasts the 100mph claim is known at all.

The late David Jenkinson, former head of education and research at the National Railway Museum, and a leading expert on the LMS, which absorbed the Lancashire & Yorkshire at the Grouping of 1923, said: "It may well have been possible for an engine with driving wheels that size to achieve a feat like that on that particular route. You can probably place some credence on it."

In his 1956 book The Lancashire & Yorkshire Railway, researcher Eric Mason wrote: "It is likely that the event will probably be regarded in the same light as the GW *City of Truro* run, because it is alleged no proper records were kept, and has in recent years been taken, rightly or wrongly, with a large pinch of salt."

Another of the 4-4-2 class – No. 1417, the test engine for Hughes' back pressure release valves – became enshrouded in "mythical legends" over its performances. Mason wrote. "Whilst there is no confirmation of an alleged 117mph near Kirkby, there is no doubt whatsoever that the engine did perform some really fast running in the capable hands of driver J Chapman of Newton Heath.

"He did all the trial work with this engine and manned her on a daily duty for many months, consisting of the 11.35am 40min express from Victoria to Liverpool, back with the 1.40pm, and then the 3.20pm semi-fast to Blackpool Central, returning home with the 6.35pm express, which was booked to run non-stop from Lytham to Salford in the comparatively easy timing of 69mins.

"The later engines so fitted, Nos. 1401, 1403, 1399 amongst them, were also very highly spoken of by drivers for their free-running qualities."

David Jenkinson commented: "The late Eric Mason was the authority on the L&Y – if he said it, it is probably reasonably authenticated."

It has also been conjectured that locomotive crews reached high speeds in defiance of speed restrictions, but played down the fact because of the fear of losing their jobs.

Across the Atlantic, it was claimed New York Central & Hudson River Railroad 4-4-0 No. 999, built to haul the 'Empire State Express', became the first in the world to travel at more than 100mph, during an exhibition run of the train on May 10, 1893, the year of its construction, although historians believe the probable maximum speed was 81mph – as recorded by observer J P Pearson, who rode on the train. Unlike *City of Truro's* feat, there are no timings showing the acceleration up to 100mph. No. 999 was preserved in 1962, and is now displayed inside the main hall at the Chicago Museum of Science and Industry.

It was also claimed Pennsylvania Railroad E2 4-4-2 No. 7002 reached 127.1mph at Crestline in Ohio while hauling its 18-hour 'Pennsylvania Special' from New York City to Chicago on June 11, 1905.

However, locomotives did not carry speedometers at the time, and speed was calculated only by measuring time

City of Truro on display at the National Railway Museum's June 2004 Railfest event, which marked both the 200th anniversary of Richard Trevithick's first public display of a railway locomotive, on the Penydarren Tramroad, near Merthyr Tydfil in 1804, and the 100th anniversary of *City of Truro's* high-speed run on Wellington Bank. ROBIN JONES

between mile markers, so the claim could not be officially substantiated.

The *New York Times* reported on June 14, 1905 that the claims published in the Chicago press had been exaggerated, and said the real speed was closer to 70–80mph.

No. 3440's unofficial record was recorded before any car or aeroplane had attained such a speed. However, the year before, an AEG experimental three-phase electric railcar near Berlin had seen 130mph reached, reportedly on October 27, 1903. It set a record for electric rail vehicles that was to last for the next 51 years.

AFTER THE RECORD

Superheating of the City class boilers was first applied to No. 3702 *Halifax* in June 1910, and all of the class, including *City of Truro*, had been fitted with superheaters by 1912.

The class were subject to the 1912 renumbering of GWR 4-4-0 locomotives. The Bulldog class was gathered together in the series 3300-3455, and other types renumbered out of that series. Accordingly, the Cities took numbers

3700-3719, previously used by Bulldogs, and *City of Truro* became No. 3717.

It was only in 1922, when the GWR, accepting that the public mood had changed, came out in the open about the 1904 record, and the Swindon empire's fabled publicity department did not hesitate in making the most of it. It would be another 12 years before LNER A3 Pacific No. 4472 *Flying Scotsman* would set an official record of 100mph.

All members of the City class were withdrawn between October 1927 and May 1931, and were scrapped, apart from one. *City of Truro*, which had continued in everyday service since its star moment, was withdrawn in March 1931, but was spared the cutter's torch because of its historical importance.

Astonishingly by today's standards, the GWR directors refused to preserve *City of Truro* at the company's expense. So GWR Chief Mechanical Engineer Charles Collett asked if it could go to the LNER's new railway museum in York.

It was donated to the rival company for preservation, and was sent from Swindon to York on March 20, 1931

Because York was thought to be a target for Luftwaffe bombers during the Second World War, *City of Truro* was moved out of the museum to the safety of the small engine shed at Sprouston station (near Kelso) on the Tweedmouth to St Boswells line in the Scottish Borders.

In 1957, *City of Truro* made a surprise but welcome comeback to the main line.

British Railways Western Region decided to return it running order and renumbered 3440, and based at Didcot shed, it hauled both normal revenue services and special excursion trains, mainly on the Didcot, Newbury and Southampton line. It was repainted into the ornate livery it carried at the time of its unofficial record in 1904.

No. 3440 was again withdrawn in 1961, and became part of the National Collection, set up by the British

Because of its historical importance, the GWR did not scrap *City of Truro* along with the rest of the City class, but donated it to its rival – LNER – for display in its then-new York Railway Museum in 1931. ROBIN JONES COLLECTION

Transport Commission to preserve key historic locomotives under statutory powers. The following year, it was taken to Swindon's former GWR Museum in Faringdon Road.

There, it was renumbered to 3717 and repainted in plain green livery with black frames.

It stayed in the museum until 1984, when it was restored for the GWR's 150th anniversary celebrations the following year. It also visited several heritage railways.

In 1989, *City of Truro* visited The Netherlands for six weeks to represent the UK and the National Railway Museum in the 150th anniversary celebrations of Dutch railways. The original choice for the visit was LNER A4 Pacific No. 4468 *Mallard*, but it failed a boiler test.

In 1990, the locomotive appeared in the National Railway Museum on Tour, an exhibition which visited Swindon in 1990, while major repairs were being carried out to the York venue, and a temporary home needed to be found for its star exhibits.

BACK ON WELLINGTON BANK 100 YEARS ON

Following a public appeal, in 2004 *City of Truro* was re-steamed yet again at a cost of £130,000 to mark the centenary of its unofficial record-breaking run.

Much of the work was undertaken by Bill Parker's Flour Mill workshop at Bream in the Forest of Dean. Retired London banker and Bodmin & Wenford railway benefactor Alan Moore stumped up the cost of overhauling the boiler at the workshop.

WR Churchward 4-4-0 No. 3440 *City of Truro* returned to passenger-carrying traffic in April 2004 – but was not finished in time for its official launch.

National Railway Museum head

Pocket-money-prized model plastic kit maker Kitmaster introduced a hugely popular self-assembly 00 scale version of *City of Truro* in the early Sixties, before the firm was taken over in 1962 by Airfix, which continued to produce the kit for decades afterwards. The mouldings were eventually acquired by Dapol, which also went on to produce the kit. ROBIN JONES COLLECTION

Andrew Scott officially relaunched the celebrity locomotive into traffic at Toddington station on the Gloucestershire Warwickshire Railway at a reception on Friday, April 2, and in public the following day. However, its first 21st-century revenue-earning train had been on Thursday, April 1, when it hauled a private charter for Chiltern Trains over the line comprising the railway's pre-war LMS inspection saloon No. 45048.

No. 3440 then returned to Wellington Bank to haul a series of main line specials, but at a speed of nowhere near 100mph.

It was the legend that is *City of Truro* that brought tens of thousands of camera-toting spectators to line the route of the Pathfinder Tours' 'Ocean Mail 100' centenary specials, headed by the overhauled 4-4-0, from Bristol Temple Meads to Kingswear on May 8 and May 10, 2004.

Inbetween, there was a stint on what is now marketed as the Dartmouth Steam Railway, hauling special trains on the actual anniversary of the reported 102.3mph run – May 9.

City of Truro successfully completed its loaded test run from Birmingham Snow Hill to Stratford-upon-Avon on Sunday, May 2, after earlier running

from Tyseley Locomotive Works to Stratford and back with its support coach.

However, the engine's support crew had experienced a few anxious moments before the 101-year-old veteran was cleared to take the first leg of its special out of Bristol Temple Meads on the Saturday. Rerailed after arriving at Barton Hill depot by low loader from Tyseley on May 6, it soon became apparent that compared to standby engine, CWR 4-6-0 No. 5029 *Nunney Castle*, the 4-4-0 was sitting down on its haunches. Adjustments to No. 3440's springs lifted frames and buffers to the correct working height, while up on the footplate a speedometer fault required attention.

Historically speaking, very few of Churchward's engines, including the 10 Cities, were fitted with speedometers, but in the modern age of paperwork and signatures for everything that moves on rails, one is judged to be critical to safety.

As a result, *City of Truro* was out and about early on the Saturday morning, departing at 7am for a test run to Weston-super-Mare and back to test it. The speedometer passed.

Given the 'tip' the 4-4-0, hauling seven coaches, 245 tons on the drawbar, got away to an excellent start, travelling down the Bristol & Exeter road to reach Taunton seven minutes early. Any hopes of attacking Wellington Bank were dispelled by a 20mph restriction through the station and for another half mile, but notwithstanding the check, No. 3440 accelerated to tackle the remainder of the 1-in-80 climb in fine style.

Once over the top, *City of Truro* continued to thrive, cruising at or around 60mph, and with favourable signals rolled into Exeter St David's early. It missed out the water stop – a brave decision some might say, considering the tender tank holds only 3500 gallons.

Setting off in glorious sunshine, No. 3440 attracted enormous crowds en route. Running easily, the 4-4-0 skirted the sea wall at Dawlish, passing Newton Abbot on time to arrive at Paignton 10 minutes ahead of its booked time. Held by signals, the train still managed to reach Kingswear two minutes to the good.

In 1958, *City of Truro* rejoined the extremely select group of historic locomotives which were taken off museum display and returned to main line duties, when the Western Region decided it wanted it back from York museum for both special tours and regular duties. It is pictured in service on May 11 that year. ROBIN JONES COLLECTION

On the Sunday, No. 3440 hauled two specials over the heritage line now known as the Dartmouth Steam Railway, the 11.15am and 2.15pm departures from Paignton to Kingswear and return. According to local reports, the number of passengers riding on the trains was equalled by lineside photographers!

The railway's general manager Barry Cogar said: "It would have been nice to have celebrated the anniversary with a fast run but there's no way we can run a 100-year-old veteran locomotive at high speed."

Station supervisor and railway author Geoffrey Kitchenside said: "It was one of those once-in-a-lifetime occasions."

Departing right time for the return trip back to Bristol, the engine had no difficulty in taking the seven coaches up the bank from Paignton, but sadly, the homeward run suffered from delays, affecting all traffic. Checked at Newton Abbot, the 'Ocean Mail 100' was pathed behind a stopper and eventually put inside at Dawlish Warren to allow two High Speed Trains to pass.

At Exeter, the heavens opened. Heavy rain, hail and thunder created a vibrant cacophony so loud it transcended the noise of trains moving in and out of St David's. While that was happening, traffic delays produced an upstaged event worth recording. A late-running First Great Western HST pulled in alongside the 'Ocean Mail' special and, coming to a halt, revealed its leading power car's nameplate: *City of Truro*!

Delayed again by service trains, No. 3440 departed Exeter five minutes down, but when given the road, took command, tackling the long climb up to Whitehall in positive fashion, the engine

entering the tunnel at 38mph. Romping downhill, but checked to 50mph on that bank, the special steamed into Taunton ahead of time. The train departed 30 minutes early.

The engine's run was cut short by a 'yellow' at Bridgwater and again at Worle Junction. By now, the train's progress was impinging on other services so control put the special inside at Yatton, where *City of Truro*'s fireman had to keep his engine quiet for 15 minutes. Given a 'green', No. 3440 took up the challenge and succeeded, bowling into platform 4 at Temple Meads, eight minutes early.

Was it a success? "Yes", said Pathfinder Tours' Richard Szwejkowski. "Of a total of 560 seats available (280 per train), 507 were occupied. Naturally, the Monday's train carried fewer passengers because of work commitments."

City of Truro subsequently hauled several specials on the national network, although because it lacked several modern safety features it was later taken out of main line service.

Afterwards, it continued to be based for several years on the Gloucestershire Warwickshire Railway, from where it visited several heritage railways.

In 2010, it took part in the GWR 175 celebrations to mark the 175th anniversary of the company, running at the Great Western Society's base at Didcot Railway Centre.

In 2013, the NRM withdrew *City of Truro* ahead of its boiler ticket expiry because of a hole being discovered in one of its tubes.

After examination it was found the locomotive required more work than first thought and was unlikely to be

As No. 3717, *City of Truro* gets a wash and brush-up before the start of the National Railway Museum's Railfest 2012 event in York in June that year, during which it hauled passenger shuttles. ROBIN JONES

operational in the foreseeable future.

In late 2015, *City of Truro* returned to STEAM – Museum of the Great Western Railway, which occupies part of the former Swindon Works, and the following year took part in Swindon 175, celebrating 175 years since the inception of Swindon as a railway town in the era of Isambard Kingdom Brunel and Daniel Gooch.

As of spring 2019, the National Railway Museum confirmed it has no plans at the present time to re-steam *City of Truro*.

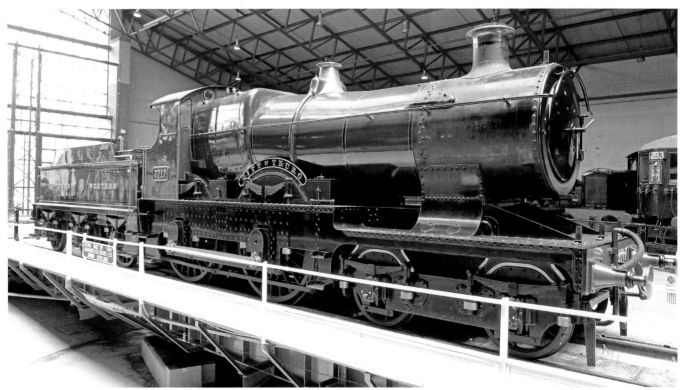

City of Truro takes a turn on the turntable in the Great Hall of the National Railway Museum at York on July 3, 2014. ROBIN JONES

Chapter 6

A locomotive LEGEND REBORN!

GWR chief mechanical engineer George Jackson Churchward revolutionised steam locomotive development with his Saint class 4-6-0s, which dated from 1902. However, this fabled name was rendered extinct in 1953 when British Railway scrapped the last one. However, a new Saint – the 78th in the series – was again pulling passenger trains in 2019, the culmination of a marathon enthusiast-led project that took more than 45 years. And the new locomotive's name is appropriately *Lady of Legend*.

The name *Lady of Legend* cannot help but conjure up a feeling of future greatness – with it becoming a no-holds-barred legendary locomotive. I have little doubt it is what it will soon become – but it ran in public for the first time only as recently as April 5, 2019.

Yet this brand-new full-size locomotive took the Great Western Society more than 45 years to build, from its inception to the first run.

Very much the new kid on the block, it is an incarnation of one of the most influential British steam types of all – the GWR 2900 or Saint class of two-cylinder passenger locomotives, designed by chief mechanical engineer George Jackson Churchward.

A total of 77 were built at Swindon between 1902/3, but the class included several variations. Most of them were built as 4-6-0s, but 13 were constructed as 4-4-2s, being converted to 4-6-0s during 1912/13, when a decision was made on the best wheel arrangement for the GWR system.

The Saints exuded Edwardian steam engineering magnificence in every way. In short, they established the design principles for GWR two-cylinder locomotive classes over the next half century. The class comprised one of the most important steps forward in railway traction of the 20th century, with ground-breaking advances in design. Indeed, Churchward's Saints are held to have influenced the whole spectrum of UK steam locomotive development.

The story began after the GWR converted the last of its Brunel 7ft¼in-broad gauge lines in 1892, and started modernising its main line network with a series of new cut-off lines to shorten its routes to the West Country, South Wales and Birmingham.

Churchward ran the rule over several experimental locomotives with different wheel arrangements and boiler designs to help him plan for the future.

Three prototype versions of the Saint were built in 1902/3 with detail differences, and each underwent trials between then and 1905. The first, No. 100, which emerged from the works in 1902, was radically different to what the Swindon empire had turned out before. Drawing upon his revolutionary principles of standardisation of design, Churchward surprised many observers with its stark modern appearance, yet few people realised the great developments that it would bring about.

The second, No. 98, was built in 1903 to a similar design but with a taper boiler, re-designed valve gear layout and cylinders and a shorter wheelbase.

No. 98 was reboilered in 1906 to

The nameplate and cabside numberplate from No. 2908 *Lady of Quality* displayed in the Didcot Railway Centre museum. ROBIN JONES

The 78th member of George Jackson Churchward's revolutionary Saint 4-6-0: No. 2999 *Lady of Legend* outside the Didcot Railway Centre locomotive shed on April 6, 2019. JAMES SHUTTLEWORTH

match the third prototype. No. 171 appeared in December 1903. With a 225psi boiler and minor amendments to the heating surface and grate area, it formed the basis of the main production series which came in 1905, when its designer was still undecided as to whether to go for a 4-6-0 or 4-4-2.

The Saint class appeared in four production series built between 1905 and 1913, each of which differed in dimensions because of the various boilers used, wheel arrangement, and arrangements for superheating, and different tenders.

The first of three prototypes for the Saint class was No. 100, built at Swindon in February 1902, and depicted in an official GWR photograph. In June 1902 it was named *Dean* (later *William Dean*) to mark the retirement of Churchward's predecessor.

Shortly after its official launch on April 5, 2019, No. 2999 heads a rake of three Edwardian coaches carrying passengers along the Didcot Railway Centre demonstration line. It was 66 years since a GW Saint 4-6-0 had hauled a train. ROBIN JONES

A LITTLE-KNOWN LEGENDARY FEAT?

It was claimed one of the new Saints – No. 2903 *Lady of Lyons* – reached 120mph during a light engine test run in May 1906. If indeed that happened, it would have placed the speed supposedly attained by the locomotive at just 6mph short of that officially obtained by LNER A4 Pacific No. 4468 *Mallard* – albeit with a loaded train – down Stoke Bank in Lincolnshire on July 3, 1938.

Yet as we saw earlier, as with *City of Truro's* 102.3mph unofficial feat on Wellington Bank, the GWR kept quiet about No. 2903's test run because of public concern over speeding trains, until a reference to the story surfaced in 1932.

Driver Henry James Robinson, whose career in transport began at the age of 14 when he drove a horse and cart, reached the rank of chief locomotive inspector of the GWR before he retired in January 1932.

Reporting his retirement, *The Times* stated that on a light engine run between Badminton and Wootton Bassett, Robinson achieved a speed of "two miles a minute".

The *Railway Magazine* invited Churchward's successor as chief mechanical engineer Charles B Collett to explain, and his response was

published in its April 1932 edition: "It appears that in May, 1906, No. 2903 – one of the newly introduced two-cylinder 4-6-0 locomotives and herself fresh from the shops – was taken for a trial run light from Swindon to Stoke Gifford, with the intention, after running the engine round the Filton-Patchway triangle, of having 'a sharp run' back.

"Signal checks were experienced, however, and No. 2903 was then stopped at Chipping Sodbury until 'line clear'

RETIREMENT OF G.W.R. CHIEF LOCOMOTIVE-INSPECTOR

Chief Locomotive-inspector Henry James Robinson is retiring on Monday after 50 years' service with the Great Western Railway Company. It is claimed that in 1906, on an experimental run with a light engine between Badminton and Wootton Bassett, he obtained a speed of two miles a minute. Mr. Robinson started work at 14 as the driver of a horse and cart. Last September, 51 years later, he helped to regain for England the world's train record for the fastest start-to-stop run. Under his supervision the "Cheltenham Flyer" express took the record from the Canadian Pacific Railway by covering the 77¼ miles between Swindon and Paddington in 59¾ minutes, an average speed of 77.9 miles an hour, and then on two successive days made even better times. Mr. Robinson was on the footplate of the Launceston Castle, which drew the train, on each occasion. Mr. Robinson has driven every member of the Royal Family. He will be succeeded by Mr. F. C. Sheldon, of Swindon.

The Times cutting from 1932 which refers to a GWR light engine run at a speed of "two miles a minute".

had been obtained through to Wootton Bassett, after which she was restarted, and there was evidently some running of very startling order down the 1-in-300 from Badminton to Little Somerford.

"The purpose of the run was to demonstrate that an engine taken straight from the shops could be run at over 100 miles per hour. Those on the footplate included Mr Collett, who was then assistant manager of the locomotive works, Mr G H Flewellen, who was the locomotive inspector, and the foreman of the erecting shop, Mr Evans. The timing for some distance by the mileposts with a stop watch was given as 120 miles per hour, and the clocking between the signalboxes of Little Somerford and Hullavington was booked as two minutes for the 4½ miles.

"Mr Collett points out that, while the object of running a new engine on its first trip at over 100 miles per hour was achieved, the timing could not be regarded as accurate and that the 102.3mph record of *City of Truro* in 1904, made under the personal observation of one of the most careful recorders of his time – the late Charles Rous-Marten – with the aid of a chronograph reading to one-fifth parts of a second, must remain the best duly authenticated railway speed record that this country has yet witnessed."

THE SAINTS SUPERSEDED

The Great Western Society has stated the Saints "represented one of the most important steps forward in railway traction of the 20th century", and they "are now acknowledged to have had a profound influence on almost every aspect of subsequent steam locomotive development".

The locomotives performed well as passenger locomotives over all the GWR long-distance and on all but the fastest express trains, but their 6ft½in driving wheels limited their usefulness on freight workings.

However, when Collett introduced the Castles in the 1920s and 30s, slowly the Saints were relegated to secondary lines. Collett worked out that a smaller-wheeled version of the Saint could become a useful mixed traffic locomotive, and he so rebuilt No. 2925 *Saint Martin* with 6ft driving wheels as the prototype of his Hall 4-6-0. Furthermore, Churchward's Saint design also became the basis for the later Modified Hall, Grange, Manor and County classes, which followed the same basis design.

The last Saint in service was No. 2920 *Saint David*. British Railways withdrew it from service in October 1953 and sent it straight for scrap, ending half a century of proud transport history at a stroke.

At the time, there was no National Collection of steam locomotives which would be set aside for posterity. Indeed, BR's 1955 Modernisation Plan, which called for all steam to be replaced by diesel and electric traction, was still two years in the future, and BR continued building steam locomotives until 1960, when Standard 9F 2-10-0 No. 92220 *Evening Star* was outshopped from Swindon.

However, the Saints had left an indelible mark on British locomotive development, and there were many who regretted their passing and the fact not one was preserved.

A 1920s view of Saint 4-6-0 No. 2908 *Lady of Quality*. ROBIN JONES COLLECTION

A hand-coloured postcard view of Saint 4-6-0 No. 2949 *Stanford Court*. ROBIN JONES COLLECTION

GWR 4-6-0 No. 2920 *Saint David* hauls empty stock into Cardiff General station from Canton Carriage Sidings, to form a train to Birmingham Snow Hill via Hereford, on July 27, 1950. When it was withdrawn and scrapped three years later, it was the last of Churchward's ground-breaking Saint class of 77 locomotives. However, 66 years later, the 78th would appear. BEN BROOKSBANK*

A HALL TO BECOME A SAINT

With modernisation of the national rail network rampant, especially in terms of withdrawing steam locomotives, many were dispatched to their nearest commercial scrapyard and cut up within days.

One glaring exception was the Woodham Brothers scrapyard on Barry Island, in South Wales.

Its operator, Dai Woodham, whose family had owned the scrapyard since the 1930s, began scrapping railway wagons in 1957 as part of the 1955 Modernisation Plan.

In 1958, he won a tender to scrap steam locomotives too, and the first batch of redundant engines arrived on March 25, 1959.

At one stage, Dai made a momentous decision. He worked out it was far more profitable to scrap redundant rolling stock and to leave the locomotives for a 'rainy day'. Bought from British Railways for their scrap value, they stood stationary on long sidings in the scrapyard, rusting away in the corrosive sea air of the Severn estuary.

To cut a long story short, his decision allowed 213 steam locomotives to be bought for preservation purposes.

His scrapyard's geographical position ensures a large proportion of the main line steam engines he bought for scrap came from the Western and Southern regions, and so we have the anomaly that while a large number of particular classes were saved for posterity, in other areas of the country, many types were rendered extinct.

Thanks to Dai Woodham, 11 Halls,

GWR 4-6-0 No. 4942 *Maindy Hall*, still in ex-Barry scrapyard condition, at Didcot Railway Centre in 2011.
BARRY LEWIS*

for instance, survived into preservation, and seven of them were returned to steam – in their own right.

Enter No. 4942 *Maindy Hall*.

Built at Swindon in July 1929, it was first allocated to Newton Abbot, and in October 1930, was transferred to Goodwick (Fishguard), and later

Swansea (Landore), Llanelli and Carmarthen. From 1936-55, it worked in the Bristol Division, being based at Weymouth, Swindon and Westbury, and eventually Bristol St Philip's Marsh, and Bath Road from December 1940 onwards.

In the summer of 1955, *Maindy Hall*

was briefly transferred to Exeter, and in September that year was switched to Banbury, working the main line between London and Birmingham Snow Hill.

Later postings were St Philips Marsh and Cardiff East dock. Ironically, as it subsequently transpired, November 1962 saw it transferred to Didcot shed, where it spent a year before withdrawal from BR service in December 1963.

Maindy Hall arrived at Woodham Brothers in June 1964.

The Great Western Society made sure many Halls survived in preservation, but one glaring omission from the heritage fleet was their predecessor, a Saint.

The society came up with a bold but in theory workable idea to retro-convert a Hall back into a Saint, and *Maindy Hall* was chosen. The aim was to reverse history: just as the original 4900 Hall class prototype of 1925 was converted from 2900 class Saint Martin, the process would therefore be authentically reversed. The purchase was completed on December 31, 1973, the day before the UK joined the European Economic Community, and 24 hours before VAT was introduced.

The society also bought No. 5900 *Hinderton Hall*, which it went on to restore in its own right.

It was decided from the outset not to turn *Maindy Hall* into a straight replica of a long-scrapped Saint, but to create the 78th member of Churchward's class, the last of which in numerical sequence had been No. 2998 *Ernest Cunard*. So it was decided the new Saint would follow on in the numbering sequence and become No. 2999. –

Saint Ivanhoe in its as-built condition as a 4-4-2, as seen in an official GWR photograph.

NUTS AND BOLTS: NEW AND OLD

While the Halls were a descendant of the Saints, back conversion to the earlier type presented formidable challenges.

The original driving wheels for the Hall were 6ft while those of a Saint were 6ft 8in, just as the Halls' front bogie wheels were 3ft and those of the Saint 3ft 2in. Clearly replacements would have to be manufactured.

Back in 1974, the railway heritage sector was still at an embryonic stage by comparison with subsequent achievements. While steam locomotives for miniature lines had continued to be built, nobody had embarked on replicating a full-size working engine. The day of new Peppercorn A1 Pacific No. 60163 *Tornado* was decades away: its construction was completed in August 2008.

The society's bold first attempt to back-convert No. 4942 was based around a rebuilt Saint with curved drop ends at the front of the frames and beneath the cab, in the style introduced from

No. 2911 onwards. Sadly, this first attempt at a Saint Project floundered because it was considered by many to be a bridge too far for the current capabilities of preservationists.

However, the mood changed with the success of the society's rebuilding of another Barry scrapyard hulk, GWR 4-6-0 No. 6023 *Edward II*.

Now carrying its distinctive British Railways early-1950s express passenger blue livery, it was considered a 'mission impossible', if only because the driving wheels had been cut at Barry – one of them is displayed at Didcot Railway Centre. If a King could be resurrected against the odds, surely it was time to look again at the Saint Project?

The first attempt to re-create a Saint was reassessed with a view to starting again. This time, it was decided to go back to the original Saint design with an inside steam pipe cylinder block, straight frames and square drop ends at the front in the style of the early Lady and Scott locomotives.

It was decided No. 2999 would include the original lever reversing gear and carry top feed, as applied progressively to the Saints from 1911. While many new parts had to be made, some genuine ones were included. They were a connecting rod from No. 2906 *Lady of Lynn* and a whistle from No. 2910 *Lady of Shalott*, while the chimney had come from a later Grange class 4-6-0.

A 'LADY' IS FOR TURNING!

No. 2999 needed a new identity, but with a title in alignment with the GWR naming policy for the Saint.

A national competition was held to choose a new name, and the judges looked for one similar to those that had been carried by the straight-frame Saints, including the 'Lady' series.

Suggested names were Lady Diana, Lady in Waiting, Lady of Lourdes, Prince Charles, Saint Dai, Phoenix and John Betjeman.

However, the winning entry was submitted by Peter Bird of Weston-super-Mare, who came up with *Lady of Legend*. In the judges' opinion it summed up the legendary spirit of the project.

Peter was presented with a full-size nameplate as his prize.

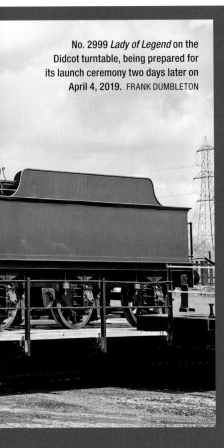

No. 2999 *Lady of Legend* on the Didcot turntable, being prepared for its launch ceremony two days later on April 4, 2019. FRANK DUMBLETON

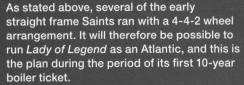

THE ATLANTIC OPTION

As stated above, several of the early straight frame Saints ran with a 4-4-2 wheel arrangement. It will therefore be possible to run *Lady of Legend* as an Atlantic, and this is the plan during the period of its first 10-year boiler ticket.

All of the Churchward Atlantics used the straight frame design. In 1904 he converted No. 171 *Albion* to a 4-4-2 in order to provide a direct comparison between the Swindon locomotive and the French De Glehn 4-4-2 *La France*. He was impressed with the result, and 13 more Atlantics were built at Swindon during 1905. Yes, they were still Saints, the only difference being the wheel arrangement.

They were considered to be 'convertible' locomotives as Churchward was by no means decided on future engine policy at this stage. In the end, the 4-6-0s were said to have had the better adhesion and all the Atlantics were so converted in 1912/13.

Before then, seven Atlantics were fitted with long-cone superheated boilers, and No. 2999 could authentically appear in this form when running as a 4-4-2. As such, No. 2999 will carry the number 191, maybe with the name Churchward or Atlantic.

Enshrouded by steam: new Saint *Lady of Legend* on the Didcot turntable prior to its official launch on May 5. ROBIN JONES

RUNNING AT LAST!

After years of eager anticipation, the official public launch of No. 2999 took place at Didcot Railway Centre on Friday, April 5, when TV presenter Prue Leith – a former member of British Rail's hotel company board – cut a ribbon as the locomotive stood in steam on the turntable.

It had taken more than 45 years from the day *Maindy Hall* was bought to the point where it ran again in public. The 51st locomotive to be bought from Dai Woodham's Barry scrapyard for preservation purposes, it became the 152nd (out of 213) to steam again…but as a completely different locomotive.

The day marked the latest pinnacle of the volunteer-led railway heritage sector, thought to have begun with the takeover of the Talyllyn Railway in 1951.

Afterwards, *Lady of Legend* gave a series of rides to guests and public visitors in a three-coach Edwardian train along the centre's demonstration line.

Its debut was followed by a steaming weekend, and on the Sunday, it was inspected by none other than Myra Blair, the granddaughter of Henry James Robinson – who as stated above, was credited with driving Saint No. 2903 *Lady of Lyons*, new from the erecting shop, at a speed well in excess of 100mph in May 1906.

Myra was accompanied by her family, which also included other descendants of Mr Robinson.

ABOVE RIGHT: TV's The Great British Bake Off star Prue Leith cuts the ribbon to unofficially launch *Lady of Legend* at 11am on April 5. Prue herself is a railway lady of legend – at his launch speech, Saint Project secretary and treasurer Richard Croucher (left) pointed out that as a member of the British Railway board, Prue was responsible for ending the much-lambasted British Rail sandwich! ROBIN JONES

RIGHT: Myra Blair (second from right) and her family giving three cheers for Henry James Robinson, said to have clocked 120mph with Saint No. 2903 *Lady of Lyons*. The members of the group are all either direct descendants of Mr Robinson, or have married into the family. FRANK DUMBLETON

Myra Blair on the footplate of 2999 *Lady of Legend* with the crew, Leigh Drew and Ali Matthews. FRANK DUMBLETON

Here's one we did earlier: many thought the restoration of part-dismembered GWR 4-6-0 No. 6023 *King Edward II* from Barry scrapyard condition was a task too great for volunteers, but the Great Western Society proved them wrong. The success and popularity of the 'Blue King' spurred on the society to restart the Saint Project. Here, *Lady of Legend* passes No. 6023 on April 6, 2019. JAMES SHUTTLEWORTH

WILL NO.2999 GO MAIN LINE?

While the conversion of *Maindy Hall* has seen the locomotive mechanically rebuilt to main line standard, it seems unlikely it will run on today's modern network.

Saint Project secretary and treasurer Richard Croucher, speaking in 2017, said: "One of the reasons why we may not run the Saint on the main line is because of the current concern about two-cylinder locomotives and gauging issues.

"It has been built to main line standard, but we have no plans to fit ETRMS (European Rail Traffic Management System) equipment to the Saint at the moment."

He said ETRMS has been fitted to No. 6023 *King Edward II*, and that repatriated GWR 4-6-0 No. 4079 *Pendennis Castle*, still under restoration at the time of writing, will be similarly equipped.

Its first year in steam will see *Lady of Legend* work at its Didcot Railway Centre birthplace, where *Maindy Hall* was last shedded in British Railways days.

Richard added: "It's probably likely that it will go out to hire on heritage lines. We would like people to come and enjoy it, and the best places are the lines in GW territory."

Chapter 7

Flying Scotsman:
THE GREATEST LEGEND OF THEM ALL

In terms of legendary locomotives, they will not rise any bigger in stature than Gresley A3 Pacific *Flying Scotsman*, whatever number it carries. Yet this ultimate defining icon of the steam area came perilously close to scrapping, or meeting its demise on the far side of the United States.

It is a statement of the obvious that British holiday resorts are at the mercy of the weather – that is the prime reason for the enormous popularity of continental breaks since package holidays became affordable to most people in the 1970s.

So why, in a week in late-March 2019, a month before the Easter holidays, and when the weather was not particularly kind on several days, was the Isle of Purbeck in Dorset suddenly packed?

Roads on the isle were busy to approaching high-season summer levels, and the car ferry from Sandbanks experienced far-longer-than-normal queues for this time of year. At the same time, Purbeck shopkeepers, cafe owners and publicans suddenly experienced a

Flying Scotsman is mobbed by fans as it stands at Swanage station on March 24. ANDREW PM WRIGHT

A3 Pacific No. 60103 Flying Scotsman heads another sell-out train towards Corfe Castle on the Swanage Railway on March 26, 2019. ANDREW PM WRIGHT

roaring trade. So what was happening?

A royal visit, perhaps? A concert by a chart-topping rock band, maybe? A mass public protest against environmental damage, like the one experienced in London a few weeks later? Or maybe someone giving out a year's supply of groceries to each visitor free of charge?

None of the above. However, we are now immersed in an age of celebrity culture, and it was indeed a larger-than-life celebrity that was wowing the crowds in Purbeck.

But whoever said that a celebrity had to be human?

This particular must-see celebrity was none other than the world's most famous steam locomotive – LNER A3 Pacific No. 60103 (previously 4472) *Flying Scotsman*… and it was booked to haul public passenger services on the Swanage Railway for five days. At the head of the first morning train, Friday, March 22, passenger numbers were said to be 'reasonable' – but the magic of television quickly changed all of that.

Broadcasting live from the line, BBC

Wherever *Flying Scotsman* travels, crowds will gather on overbridges and every other nearby vantage point, as at Swanage on March 24, 2019, such is its overriding popularity. ANDREW PM WRIGHT

South TV and BBC Radio Solent caught the public's imagination and suddenly railway officials were swamped by the public demanding to buy tickets to ride.

Penny Vaudoyer, the daughter of the late Alan Pegler, who bought the A3 out of British Railways service in 1963, flew in from Portugal to flag off the first train.

As the morning wore on roads to Swanage began to become markedly far busier than normal for the time of year, well before any semblance of the holiday season had begun.

At Poole, delays of more than an hour on the Sandbanks ferry were reported

by Radio Solent, which also described traffic from north Bournemouth, Ferndown and Wimborne areas building up on the Upton bypass leading to Wareham, Corfe Castle and beyond.

Beezer Buses ran extra services from Bournemouth and Poole, while in Swanage, several roads were closed to prevent traffic jams and to protect pedestrians making for the station.

Crowd control and safety was carried by railway personnel and a private security company.

As word spread, demand for tickets to ride on the five seven-coach trains kept

railway officials busy coping with the sheer volume of public demand during the March 22-26 running period,

On the Sunday, a drone was spotted flying illegally over the railway.

During those five days, trains were filled to 97% capacity, with 8640 seats sold.

Flying Scotsman was then placed on static display at Corfe Castle station – and again, its celebrity status went into overdrive.

Another 5485 visitors paid to board the footplate and walk through the locomotive tender corridor to view repatriated Pullman Car 14, which ran behind *Flying Scotsman* during its ill-fated trip of North America between 1969-72, as described further on.

Meanwhile, shops, pubs and restaurants in Corfe Castle, the picture-postcard village dominated by the ruins of its medieval castle, saw a sudden and unexpected pre-season upsurge in trade, despite periods of heavy rain that beset the Purbeck countryside.

The Swanage Railway's business division director Mick Gould, a volunteer signalman and train guard of the line, said: "The number of people that wanted to ride behind and see the iconic *Flying Scotsman* exceeded our expectations, proving No. 60103 is still the nation's favourite steam locomotive and truly the peoples' engine.

"So many people worked tirelessly and beyond the call of duty for both the planning and execution of what was the largest and most challenging special event in the history of the Swanage Railway.

"It was a tremendous event and

Bound for the 'Sunny South': No. 60103 *Flying Scotsman* and its support coach head through Deeping St James, between Spalding and Peterborough, during its movement to the Swanage Railway on March 18, 2019. ROBIN JONES

seeing the smiles on so many peoples' faces during the event was wonderful.

"No. 60103 is a marvellous machine and part of this country's engineering DNA. *Flying Scotsman* is a working museum. It is open to the public and has a magic of its own. It has created a huge atmosphere, a huge amount of excitement.

"If you bring *Flying Scotsman* to a railway line, especially a branch line, you are bound to get crowds of people willing to buy tickets, and a heritage railway like the Swanage Railway needs revenue – it can't run on love, unfortunately.

"It is a huge morale boost for the volunteers here as well, especially the drivers who can sit in the cab. A lot of planning goes into an event like this."

Once its landmark crowd-pulling visit was completed, *Flying Scotsman* and its main line support coach departed the railway via Wareham on Friday, April 12, heading for Southall depot.

On arrival, the 4-6-2 ran around its coach, then having coupled up, headed for Southall, where it stopped overnight before heading to York the following day.

Arriving at its owner's (National Railway Museum) north siding, 'Scotsman' was part of the attraction of the venue's Easter week programme – where again, the crowds turned out to see the green machine.

However, the journey back up north from Purbeck was not without incident.

National newspapers reported that on April 12, footage posted on the internet appeared to show another drone observing *Flying Scotsman*, but

Flying Scotsman stands outside Swanage signalbox on March 19, 2019 ANDREW PM WRIGHT

this time flying dangerously close to the locomotive as it passed between Farnborough and Woking in Surrey.

Had it hit the locomotive, the drone could have damage to vital equipment, costing thousands to repair and causing hours of train delays…or maybe worse.

The incident sparked an investigation by both Network Rail and British Transport Police, with a warning offenders could be taken to court and fined up to £2500.

The incident harked back to another a month after the completion of Flying Scotsman's last overhaul in February 2016. While visiting the North Yorkshire Moors Railway, a drone hit a tree causing the camera to fall off and crash into one of eight carriages as the A3 ran near Grosmont.

However, more disdain for public

safety was to follow on Sunday, May 5, when No. 60103 was heading the final (Scarborough to Paddington) leg of the Railway Touring Company's 'Great Britain XII' annual marathon rail cruise.

Trespassers who threw caution to the winds to get a closer glimpse of the celebrity green machine stood next to the 125mph running line – causing both *Flying Scotsman* (also delayed earlier by a broken rail) and 56 regular passenger trains to be held up, for a total of 1000 minutes.

At one stage, eight CrossCountry trains were brought to a standstill because of the trespass. One train driver claimed he had seen trespassers every 200 yards.

British Transport Police (BTP) released a photograph of two people standing next to the line in Elford,

Flying Scotsman at Corfe Castle station on March 19, 2019. ANDREW PM WRIGHT

THE ORIGIN OF THE 'FLYING SCOTSMAN'

Confusion often arises in the general media between *Flying Scotsman* the locomotive and the train of the same name.

The express passenger train service that operates from London to Edinburgh under that banner dates back to 1860.

The three railway companies that ran services over what became known as the East Coast Main Line – the Great Northern, the North Eastern and the North British Railways – set up the East Coast Joint Stock pool of carriages

for through services, using common vehicles, so passengers no longer had to change en route between the two capital cities. In 1862, the first 'Special Scotch Express' ran, with simultaneous departures at 10am from the GNR's King's Cross terminus and the North British Railway's Edinburgh Waverley. The original journey took 10½ hours, but increasing competition from the rival West Coast route from Euston via Crewe and Carlisle to Glasgow and Edinburgh (run by the London & North Western

An LNER poster promoting 'The Flying Scotsman' train in 1935.

and the Caledonian railways) and improvements in railway technology saw this time cut to 8½ hours by 1888.

From the 1870s, the train was unofficially known as the 'Flying Scotsman', but the year after the Grouping of 1923, it was officially adopted as the title of the train by the newly formed London & North Eastern Railway.

Portrayed hauling the 'Flying Scotsman' train through Hatfield in Edwardian times, Great Northern Railway No. 990 *Henry Oakley* was built at Doncaster in 1898 and became the first 4-4-2 in Britain. It was the only locomotive on the GNR to carry a name (in honour of the general manager of the railway) until 1922, when Gresley's Pacifics were introduced. ROBIN JONES COLLECTION

A3 Pacific No. 60103 *Flying Scotsman* departs Corfe Castle on April 12 with the village's medieval castle ruins in the background. An encounter with a drone in Surrey later that day would generate national newspaper headlines. ANDREW PM WRIGHT

THE MAN WHO BUILT A LEGEND

On June 19, 1876, Herbert Nigel Gresley was born in Dublin Street, Edinburgh, the youngest of five children of the Rev Nigel Gresley, rector of Netherseal, in Derbyshire, and his wife Joanna Beatrice.

In 1893, young Nigel left Marlborough College and became apprenticed to Francis Webb at the London & North Western Railway's Crewe locomotive works.

Five years later, he moved across to the Lancashire & Yorkshire Railway, and gained experience in the drawing office.

He was appointed as running shed foreman at Blackpool in 1900, and later graduated to becoming assistant manager at Newton Heath carriage works.

In 1901, Gresley married Ethel Francis Fullagar.

He was appointed as carriage and wagon superintendent of the Great Northern Railway in 1905, after a stint as assistant to the L&Y's equivalent.

In 1911, Gresley superseded H A Ivatt as the Great Northern Railway chief mechanical engineer. He began drawing plans for a locomotive type that would better the company's Ivatt large-boilered Atlantics, and he looked at the American 4-6-2s, a wheel arrangement known also as Pacifics.

Four year later, in 1915, Gresley produced plans for a longer version of the successful GNR Ivatt Atlantic design with four cylinders. He then changed tack somewhat, and analysed in depth what was a far better arrangement, that of the Pennsylvania Railroad's K4 Pacific, the first of which had appeared the year before.

Gresley adopted aspects of the K4 blueprint to design a modern Pacific.

However, he did not invent the first British Pacific. In 1908, the Great Western Railway's George Jackson Churchward oversaw the production of No. 111 *The Great Bear*, a unique company flagship locomotive, which proved a disappointment. Sadly, it did not survive long enough to enter the National Collection.

Gresley's first three-cylinder 2-8-0 was built in 1918, incorporating

Nigel Herbert Gresley, the man who gave the world *Flying Scotsman*.

conjugated valve gear, and two years later, because of his work in munitions at Doncaster Works, he was awarded the CBE for his wartime services. The same year, his first three-cylinder 2-6-0 was outshopped, later to become the LNER K3 class.

The likes of *The Great Bear* would not be seen again in the UK until 1922, when Gresley built his first pair of three-cylinder Pacifics for the GNR – Nos. 1470 *Great Northern* and 1471 *Sir Frederick Banbury*.

The railway company board was so impressed with them they commissioned another 10.

When the GNR became part of the new LNER at the Grouping only months later, the 10 were being built in Doncaster Works.

The LNER kept Gresley on as its chief mechanical engineer, and adopted his A1 Pacific design as the standard express passenger locomotive for the LNER main line, and a total of 51 were built between 1923-25.

It was his third Pacific that concerns us here. GNR No. 1472 (numbered 4472 by the LNER) emerged from Doncaster Works on February 7, 1923, as serial number 1564.

It was the first locomotive to carry

Staffordshire, both with cameras and one having mounted a tripod a few feet from the nearest rail, and immediately appealed to the public to identify them.

It was revealed BTP were being deployed on all main line Flying Scotsman trains in an increased bid to identify and apprehend all such offenders.

Furthermore, the National Railway Museum said that video cameras had been fitted to the locomotive in order to help prepare cases against trespassers for prosecution.

At one stage, Network Rail stated that the locomotive could even be banned from running on the main line if such a drastic step was needed to ensure safety.

So what is the seemingly immortal, infinite and unabated appeal of *Flying Scotsman*, widely regarded as the most legendary locomotive of them all, that leads many people to take huge risks to view it at all costs?

The first of Nigel Gresley's Pacifics: A1 No. 1470 *Great Northern*. The third would be No. 1472 *Flying Scotsman*. ROBIN JONES COLLECTION

LNER No. 1472 (later 4472) at Belle Isle, near King's Cross, with a northbound express in 1923. NRM

the LNER's famous apple green livery – the same shade as GNR green – but without the dark red frames, and without the additional dark green border on the tender.

On February 22, No. 1472 was displayed at Marylebone and entered service two days later, allocated to Doncaster shed. Initially, the Pacifics were too long for the turntable at King's Cross and had to run to Ferme Park to turn. They only had two regular daily turns to the capital for their first few months.

During a general repair at Doncaster in February 1924, No. 1472 became No. 4472 and was named *Flying Scotsman*, making the locomotive synonymous with what had by then become the world's most-famous train. Subsequent locomotives of the class were named after winners at Doncaster horse races.

To publicise the newly officially named train, *Flying Scotsman* was displayed at the British Empire Exhibition at Wembley from May to November 1924, alongside Great Western Railway Castle 4-6-0 No. 4079 *Pendennis Castle*, which the GWR claimed to be "the most powerful steam engine in Britain".

Gresley presented a paper to the Institution of Mechanical Engineers on three-cylinder locomotive design in 1925. Meanwhile, interchange trials with GWR Castles took place, leading to major improvements to the A1 design. No. 4472 was again displayed at the Wembley exhibition to mark the centenary of the world's first public steam-hauled railway, the Stockton & Darlington. The *Flying Scotsman* legend was born.

Flying Scotsman was one of the star exhibits at the now-legendary British Empire Exhibition at Wembley in 1924. NRM

The Flying Scotsman is a 1929 black and white part-silent film set on the 'Flying Scotsman' train from London to Edinburgh – and had No. 4472 in a starring role. It was notable for its daring stunts performed aboard the moving train. Pictured is actress Pauline Johnson walking along the edge of the locomotive, a genuine stunt in the climax of the film.

FIRST NON-STOP RUN FROM KING'S CROSS TO EDINBURGH

Gresley was elected president of the Association of Railway Locomotive Engineers in 1926, such was the reputation he had by then acquired.

The following year, his A1s were scheduled to work non-stop from King's Cross to Newcastle with the 9.50am 'Relief Scotsman' in the summer timetable. The first such train was worked by No. 4475 *Flying Fox.*

July 1927 saw Gresley's A1s start being upgraded to A3s with No. 4480 *Enterprise.* The cylinder diameter was reduced from 20in to 19in, the superheater expanded to 43 elements, and most importantly, the boiler pressure increased from 180llbs to 220lbs.

The same year, Gresley introduced his D49 4-4-0 as a new intermediate express passenger locomotive. Production began of the new A3 'Super Pacifics' in 1928. The first appeared on August 22, and Gresley's plan was to convert all A1s into A3s as and when they entered the works for overhaul.

Flying Scotsman, which was still an A1 at the time, had a corridor tender supplied to it on April 11, and was reallocated to King's Cross shed. Following the valve gear modifications, the A1s' coal consumption was drastically reduced, and it became possible to run the London to Scotland service non-stop with a heavy train on one tender full of coal.

That meant the LNER could better the eight hours 15 minutes that had been agreed with the West Coast rivals following the end of the last 'Race to the North' in late-Victorian times..

Ten A1s and their improved successors – the A3s – were designated for use on the 'Flying Scotsman' train, including No. 4472.

They were each given corridor

Flying Scotsman leaves Wood Green Tunnel with a Grantham to King's Cross express on its first trip after its appearance at the 1925 Wembley exhibition.

tenders (each with a coal capacity of nine tons instead of eight) to circumvent footplate crew fatigue by enabling a replacement driver and fireman to take over halfway without stopping the train.

The new train had improved catering and other on-board services, including the introduction of a barber's shop.

No. 4472 was selected to haul the first of its namesake train's non-stop runs over the 392 miles from King's Cross to Edinburgh on May 1, 1928, and it achieved it with flying colours in eight hours and three minutes.

It would be the first of many adventures that would bring a sackful of accolades to No. 4472.

Back then, it was a record time for a scheduled service, but its London Midland & Scottish Railway rival had stolen a march four days earlier, running the 'Royal Scot' non-stop the 399 miles from Euston to Edinburgh, as a one-off publicity stunt.

The following year, No. 4472 appeared in the film The Flying Scotsman, enhancing its fame still further.

Following valve gear modifications, the A1 locomotive's coal consumption was drastically reduced and it was thus found possible to run the service non-stop with a heavy train on one

tender full of coal. That meant the LNER could better the eight hours 15 minutes that had been agreed with the West Coast rivals following the end of the last Race to the North in 1895.

THE 100MPH WORLD RECORD – NOW OFFICIAL 30 YEARS ON!

In 1932 Gresley rejected an offer to replace Sir Henry Fowler as the chief mechanical engineer of the LMS, and William Stanier from the GWR was given the job instead.

In 1934, while Gresley's first P2 express passenger 2-8-2, No. 2001 *Cock o' the North*, was completed, he looked at the new German high-speed diesel train the 'Flying Hamburger', but concluded that steam remained the premier form of motive power, at least for the moment – and a golden moment was indeed just around the corner

We saw earlier how GWR 4-4-0 No. 3440 *City of Truro* probably reached 102.3mph in 1904, but the timings were never verified as official.

However, on November 30, 1934, driven by Bill Sparshatt and running a test train down Stoke Bank on the East Coast Main Line, near Little Bytham, in Lincolnshire, *Flying Scotsman* became the first locomotive to be officially recorded as having reached 100mph, and earned a place in the land speed record for railed vehicles.

No. 4472 had that day made not only the fastest long-distance run on any British railway, but probably the fastest journey of its length ever made by steam. A four-coach train was hauled over the 185.8 miles from King's Cross to Leeds in 152 minutes, and six coaches were worked back in 157 minutes on the same day.

The 250-mile round trip was covered at an average of 80mph, with 40 miles at an average of 90mph, and for a distance of 600 yards, the headline-grabbing 100mph.

The publicity conscious LNER was only too happy to make as much as possible out of No. 4472's feat, setting *Flying Scotsman* on the railroad to immortality.

In a similar test run from London to Newcastle and back, A3 No. 2750

No. 4472 *Flying Scotsman*, then still an A1, departs King's Cross with the 'Flying Scotsman' in 1932. That year, the journey time for the 'Flying Scotsman' train was reduced to seven hours 30 minutes, and by 1938 cut to seven hours 20 minutes. ROBIN JONES COLLECTION

Flying Scotsman passes Sandy in Bedfordshire on May 1, 1937. ROBIN JONES COLLECTION

Papyrus reached 108mph on Stoke Bank on March 25, 1935, a world record for a non-streamlined steam locomotive.

However, a glamorous new LNER was waiting in the wings.

On September 30, the first Gresley streamlined A4 Pacific – No. 2509 *Silver Link* – entered service in spectacular fashion on the 'Silver Jubilee'.

And on July 3 ,1938, sister No. 4468 *Mallard* set a world steam railway record of 126mph, also on Stoke Bank, during breaking trials.

That record has never been officially broken.

In January 1935, the last of the A3 class to be built – No. 2508 *Brown Jack* – was outshopped from Doncaster Works. Gresley's A1/A3 class now totalled 78 engines.

In 1936, Gresley was knighted, and was also awarded an honorary D.Sc by Manchester University. The same year, the first of his V 2-6-2s – No. 4771 *Green Arrow* – made its debut.

Finally looking at electric traction as a successor to steam, that year Gresley began design work on trans-Pennine electrification.

RINGING THE CHANGES

No. 4472 ran with its corridor tender between April 1928 and October 1936, after which it reverted to the original type. In July 1938, it was paired with a streamlined non-corridor tender, and ran with this type until withdrawal.

Gresley died suddenly from a heart attack on April 5, 1941, and a memorial service was held in Chelsea's Old Parish Church four days later. His successor as chief mechanical engineer was Edward Thompson.

In the spring of 1943, No. 4472 emerged from Doncaster Works in wartime black livery.

In April 1945, the 17 remaining unrebuilt A1s, including No. 4472, were reclassified as A10s, because the new LNER Peppercorn Pacifics were to be classified A1.

May 1, 1945 saw the first Gresley A1 – No. 4470 *Great Northern* – enter Doncaster Works for rebuilding by Thompson into the prototype A1/1, a move seen by some as an insult to Gresley's memory.

On January 20, 1946, Thompson's renumbering scheme saw No. 4472

briefly become No. 502 and then on May 5, No. 103.

Finally, on November 18, 1946, *Flying Scotsman* re-entered Doncaster for upgrading to A3, and was given a boiler from No. 2576 *The White Knight*. 'Scotsman' underwent its most extensive rebuild until 1996. The major modification included a boiler with the long 'banjo' dome, of the type that it carries today.

On January 4, 1947, *Flying Scotsman* re-entered traffic in post-war Thompson LNER apple green livery.

Nationalisation took place on January 1, 1948, when the 'Big Four' companies became part of the new British Railways.

Flying Scotsman became No. E103 that March, and No. 60103 in December that year.

December 16, 1949, saw *Flying Scotsman* outshopped in the new but short-lived BR express passenger blue. The livery was found to be impractical as it couldn't easily be touched up at works overhauls.

On March 14, 1952, *Flying Scotsman* was repainted in BR Brunswick green, based on GWR passenger locomotive livery, and was adopted as standard for express and passenger locomotives, in view of the problems experienced with the earlier blue express livery.

Flying Scotsman had been reallocated to Leicester shed on June 4, 1950 for working services to Marylebone, and on November 15, 1952, it returned to East Coast Main Line service, allocated to Grantham for four years, except for a short period at King's Cross in the summer of 1954.

It was normal practice for locomotives to be changed on ECML expresses at Grantham, with the exception of long-distance non-stop trains, which were all in the hands of the corridor-tendered A4 Pacifics.

In April 1954, No. 60103 was converted to left-hand drive during an overhaul at Doncaster.

Flying Scotsman was reallocated to King's Cross shed on April 7, 1957, where it remained until withdrawal.

In December 1958, a Kylchap double blastpipe and chimney were fitted to No. 60103 as part of a programme to upgrade the entire A3 class. The double chimneys cost £153 per engine, and brought about a reduction in coal consumption of 1b per mile, but the downside was soft exhaust and smoke drift that tended to obscure the driver's forward vision.

A solution was found in the form of German-type smoke deflectors, which were fitted to the class from 1960, radically changing the A3s' appearance, and this is how No. 60103 looks today, its deflectors having been fitted in December 1961. Only 55 A3s received the deflectors.

Nigel Gresley congratulates the crew of *Flying Scotsman* at the end of its November 30, 1934 trip, in which the locomotive officially reached 100mph on Stoke Bank in Lincolnshire. NRM

The A3s then began to be used throughout on King's Cross to Newcastle trains, and were considered the equal of the A4s.

In 1958, BR's first main line diesel locomotives arrived on the East Coast Main Line in the form of a handful of 2000hp English Electric Type 4s, later to become Class 40 – and on December 7, No. 60104 *Solaria* became the first A3 to be withdrawn by BR, from King's Cross shed, as a result of accident damage.

In 1960, the Deltic – later Class 55 – diesels began operating on the East Coast Main Line, posing the first real threat to the Gresley Pacifics' 40-year domination of the route.

The list of locomotives to be scheduled for preservation by the British Transport Commission as part of the National Collection was published in 1961, and astonishingly, when its subsequent mass popularity is taken into account, omitted *Flying Scotsman*.

In 1962, with other class members still operating on express passenger work, BR announced it would scrap *Flying Scotsman*.

January 15, 1963 saw *Flying Scotsman* make its last run, the 1.15pm from King's Cross to Leeds, as far as Doncaster. It was withdrawn by BR, with 2,076,000 miles on the clock.

A group called Save Our Scotsman hurriedly drew up plans to buy No. 4472, but in those early days of railway preservation, were unable to raise the £3000 asking price, the scrap value of the locomotive.

However, it was announced businessman Alan Pegler, who in 1954 saved the Ffestiniog Railway, had bought *Flying Scotsman* for £3000, and took possession of it on April 16, 1963.

In 1961, Pegler had received £70,000 for his shareholding when Northern Rubber, a company started by his grandfather, was sold to Pegler's Valves.

With spare cash on his hands, he stepped in and bought *Flying Scotsman* outright from British Railways. The first train that ran under his ownership was from Paddington to Ruabon, four days later: it was *Flying Scotsman's* first trip

Ffestiniog Railway saviour and businessman Alan Pegler stands on the front of *Flying Scotsman* at King's Cross in 1963 after buying it from British Railways, following the failure of an earlier enthusiast-led attempt to save it. NRM

Flying Scotsman heads a train comprising LNER Gresley teak coaches. ROBIN JONES COLLECTION

into Wales. On June 16, regular steam working on the GN main line into King's Cross ended, and November 16 saw A4 No. 60009 *Union of South Africa* haul BR's last official steam train out of the terminus. Also in 1964, A3 Pacific No. 60106 *Flying Fox* headed the final steam-hauled 'Flying Scotsman' into

King's Cross, after the rostered Deltic failed. The last A3 to be withdrawn was No. 60052 *Prince Palatine* in January 1966, from St Margaret's shed Edinburgh. When No. 60041 *Salmon Trout* was scrapped in 1966, *Flying Scotsman* became the sole surviving Gresley non-streamlined Pacific.

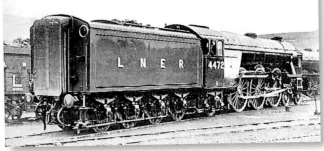

Flying Scotsman fitted with a corridor tender in 1928.

LEFT: No. 60103 *Flying Scotsman* at King's Cross on April 10, 1961, waiting to depart with 'The Tees-Thames', minus those latter-day BR German-style smoke deflectors. ROBIN JONES COLLECTION

All set and ready to roll: *Flying Scotsman* prepared with US-style cowcatcher in 1969 in readiness for its North American tour. B MILNES*

LEFT: 'Devon Belle' Pullman observation carriage Car 14 running behind *Flying Scotsman* on its ill-fated tour of North America. The A3 ran again with Car 14 during its 2019 visit to Swanage. PENNY VAUDOYER

A SECOND LIFE ON THE NATIONAL NETWORK

Pegler ploughed much of his money into having the locomotive restored at its Doncaster Works birthplace, as closely as possible to its LNER condition, in that company's livery.

The German-style smoke deflectors were removed, the double chimney was replaced by a single chimney, and once again No. 4472 – to which *Flying Scotsman* reverted – was paired with a corridor tender.

He then convinced the British Railways board to allow him to use *Flying Scotsman* for enthusiasts' specials, including on May 1, 1968, the 40th anniversary run of its non-stop London to Edinburgh feat.

Modernisation saw facilities for serving steam locomotives being ripped out all over the system, so in 1966 he bought a second corridor tender for use as an extra water carrier. It came from No. 60009 *Union of South Africa*.

Its first passenger trip with both tenders was from Lincoln to Blackpool that October, and a fortnight later, No. 44762 became the first steam engine to work out of King's Cross since BR's last official train of June 1967 saw No. 4472 head a run to mark the 40th anniversary of the non-stop run from King's Cross to Newcastle, but it did not achieve a non-stop run.

However, on May 1, 1968, *Flying Scotsman* successfully restaged the 40th anniversary of its London to Edinburgh non-stop run, in seven hours and 45 minutes, and repeated it southbound four days later.

After British Rail imposed a ban on steam haulage after the legendary '15 Guinea Special' on August 11, 1968, No. 4472 was the only steam locomotive permitted to run on the national network.

THE NORTH AMERICAN DISASTER

On August 31, 1969, *Flying Scotsman* worked its last railtour in Britain under Pegler's contract with BR, which was valid until 1971.

In readiness for a planned exhibition train tour of North America, it was fitted with a bell and cowcatcher for its run from King's Cross to Newcastle, to comply with US railroad regulations.

On September 19, No. 4472 and a set of Pullman coaches were shipped from Liverpoool docks across the Atlantic to embark on a highly ambitious tour of Canada and the USA, devised by Pegler to promote British goods and services, and backed by Harold Wilson's Labour government.

In the USA, No. 4472 was also equipped with buckeye couplings, American-style whistle, air brakes, and high-intensity headlamp.

The tour began on October 8 in Boston, Massachusetts, and ran to New York, Washington and Dallas in 1969, from Texas to Wisconsin and Montreal in 1970, and from Toronto to San Francisco in 1971, a total of 15,400 miles. The latter trip, in September 1971, made for a British Week exhibition, proved to be a financial disaster, and left Pegler bankrupt and £132,000 in debt.

The plug on the Labour government's financial support for the tour had been pulled by Edward Heath's Conservative Government in 1970. Yet Pegler carried on with the trip regardless.

The locomotive ended up being stored at a US army depot in California to keep it out of the reach of angry creditors.

Pegler was by then so broke he had to earn his fare home to Britain in 1971 by working his passage on a P&O cruise ship as an on-board entertainer, giving lectures about trains and how steam engines worked.

So eight years after he saved *Flying Scotsman* from the scrapman, this British transport 'treasure of treasures' was facing the threat of a similar fate again.

SIR WILLIAM SAVED IT FOR KEEPS

In August 1972, the A3 ended up in storage at a US army base at Stockton, near Sacramento, in California.

In stepped multi-millionaire enthusiast William McAlpine, a director of the construction company Sir Robert McAlpine.

He bought *Flying Scotsman* for £25,000, direct from the finance company that had seized it, and returned it to Britain, the A3 being loaded aboard the *MV California Star* at Oakland Docks, California, on January 19, 1973.

Flying Scotsman arrived back at Liverpool docks in February 1973, and it ran under its own steam to Derby works, where Sir William paid for it to be overhauled.

In the summer of 1973, the A3 ran on what is now known as the Dartmouth Steam Railway.

LEFT: Complete with its Pegler-era two tenders, *Flying Scotsman* heads through Kansas in this postcard view. ROBIN JONES COLLECTION

Flying Scotsman at Fisherman's Wharf, San Francisco, in March 1972. DREW JACKSON

Flying Scotsman at Carnforth in 1982 with original single chimney and without the later German-style smoke deflectors. DAVID INGHAM*

On August 10, 1974, No. 4472 was relocated to the Steamtown museum at Carnforth, back then a popular bolthole for preservation, and which became its base for a series of main line tours.

August 31, 1975, saw the A3 take part in the Stockton & Darlington 150 cavalcade at Shildon, and the month afterwards, it ran on its former happy hunting ground of the East Coast Main Line, between York and Shildon, for the first time since 1969.

In December 1977, *Flying Scotsman* entered the Vickers Engineering Works in Barrow-in-Furness for heavy repairs,

including the fitting of the boiler from A4 No. 60019 *Bittern*.

On March 12, 1980, No. 4472 headed the first steam train out of Liverpool Lime Street since August 11, 1968, as part of the Liverpool & Manchester Railway 150th anniversary celebrations. It also starred in the Rocket 150 cavalcade at Rainhill on May 24-26.

On February 27, 1983, to mark its 60th birthday, No. 4472 had its first run on the GN main line since 1969, from Peterborough to York.

The trip was repeated on the following two Sundays. Special

authorisation was given by BR for the use of this route, but it was not felt this could be extended to King's Cross.

In a foretaste of worse to come in future times, trespass by members of the public gave serious cause for concern, and resulted in no further East Coast Main Line runs and no further inter-city routes being authorised for steam running.

November 20, 1984, saw *Flying Scotsman* haul a Royal Train conveying HM The Queen Mother from Stratford to North Woolwich for the opening of the new museum at the station.

SETTING NEW RECORDS DOWN UNDER

Despite the abject failure of its former owner's North American tour, No. 4472 was booked to take part in Australia's bi-centennial celebrations in 1988, in place of the requested *Mallard*, 50 years after the A4's world steam record run.

Accordingly, it was shipped from Tilbury docks on September 11.

Down Under, *Flying Scotsman* headed a series of railtours, including a return transcontinental run from Sydney via Alice Springs.

In doing so, it became the first steam locomotive to travel on the new Central Australia Railway.

It broke the Australian steam speed record by hitting 84mph on a run from Benalla to Seymour.

In Perth, after running unassisted with 780 tons across the Nullarbor Plain, it was reunited with GWR 4-6-0 No. 4079 *Pendennis Castle*, which had stood alongside *Flying Scotsman* at the Wembley exhibition of 1924, and which had been sold by William McAlpine to an Australian mining company.

In 2000, *Pendennis Castle* returned to Britain and passed into the ownership of the Great Western Society at Didcot Railway Centre.

On August 8, 1989, *Flying Scotsman* set another record en route to Alice Springs from Melbourne, when it ran from Parkes to Broken Hill non-stop, the longest such run by a steam locomotive

recorded anywhere in the world.

That tour also saw No. 4472 better its own haulage record, heading a 735-ton train over the 490 miles between Tarcoola and Alice Springs.

No. 4472 arrived back at Tilbury on December 14, 1989. Its main line ticket expired in 1993, leaving it to run only on heritage railways.

On July 22, following overhaul by Babcock Robey Ltd, *Flying Scotsman* reappeared with a double chimney, Kylchap blastpipe and smoke deflectors, in BR Brunswick green as No. 60103.

Its first runs in this guise were on what is now marketed as the Dartmouth Steam Railway, between Paignton and Kingswear.

On its first passenger trip in Australia from Melbourne to Albury, *Flying Scotsman* speeds towards Broadford on October 25, 1988. During its successful and record-breaking tour Down Under, it was equipped with electric lighting and air brakes for operation on Australian railways. BRIAN SHARPE

The late pharmaceuticals entrepreneur Dr Tony Marchington in the cab of *Flying Scotsman* when it was still in grey primer, prior to its 1999 relaunch. ROBIN JONES

BACK IN PUBLIC OWNERSHIP – WHERE IT SHOULD HAVE BEEN ALL ALONG

On September 21, 1993, *Flying Scotsman* passed into the ownership of a consortium, which included McAlpine, by then Sir William McAlpine, and famous record producer Pete Waterman, himself a former British Railways worker and a major enthusiast in his own right.

Sadly, by 1995, No. 4472 was in pieces at Southall depot, without the necessary finance to return it to the main line condition.

The following year, the late pharmaceuticals entrepreneur Dr Tony Marchington bought it for £1.25million, and over the next three years spent £1m on restoring it under the helm of engineer Roland Kennington.

In 1999, it underwent several night-time test runs in grey primer livery, before it was repainted in LNER apple green livery.

Minus the smoke deflectors, its comeback run on July 4, 1999, drew massive crowds alongside the East Coast Main Line as it ran from King's Cross to York.

A police spokesman estimated "one million people" turned out to watch it

Alan Pegler alongside *Flying Scotsman* at the opening of the Railfest 2004 event at the National Railway Museum. ROBIN JONES

Following its £1million rebuild under Dr Tony Marchington, *Flying Scotsman* prepares to depart King's Cross with its comeback run on July 4, 1999. Tony is seen standing on the front of the locomotive in a scene reminiscent of Alan Pegler's purchase of the locomotive 36 years before. ROBIN JONES

from the lineside, and the writer himself saw many people who should have known better standing on the wrong side of the trackside fence, one with a young girl on his shoulders.

Marchington drew up plans for a Flying Scotsman Village, firstly at a site near Ambergate, in Derbyshire, and then in Edinburgh, and Flying Scotsman plc was floated on the junior stock exchange OFEX.

However, Edinburgh City Council rejected the plans, and in September 2003, Marchington was declared bankrupt. In October 2003, the company announced losses of £474,619, and said it did not have sufficient finance to trade after April 2004, and its shares were suspended from OFEX.

Heritage Railway magazine subsequently found *Flying Scotsman* was being quietly offered for sale through a luxury second-hand car dealership.

In February 2004, a debt agency acting on behalf of Flying Scotsman plc announced a sealed bid auction for the locomotive in early April.

Again, fears were the world's most famous locomotive might be sold abroad, never to return.

The National Railway Museum successfully bid £2.31m on behalf of the National Collection, the money coming from a nationwide public appeal, a £1.8 million grant from the National

Heritage Memorial Fund, £70,000 raised by the Yorkshire Post, and Virgin Trains founder Richard Branson matching the £350,000 in public donations. This was ironic as half a century earlier the NRM had declined to protect *Flying Scotsman* from the scrapman, despite its historic achievements and legendary status.

The sale included the spare A3 boiler used by No. 4472 from 1965-78.

Serenaded by pipers, *Flying Scotsman* made a triumphant entry in York to open the museum's hugely successful Railfest 2004 event, which marked 200 years since Cornish mining engineer Richard Trevithick gave the first public demonstration of a steam locomotive.

Afterwards, it re-entered service on the main line, hauling charter trips, including the 'Scarborough Spa Express'. However, its poor mechanical condition resulted in several failures and heavy repair bills.

This time round, *Flying Scotsman* last steamed on December 20, 2005, after hauling a series of Christmas dining trips from Tyseley Locomotive works in Birmingham.

The National Railway Museum then began overhauling the A3 in its York workshops, with the aim of returning *Flying Scotsman* to its original specification.

It was estimated the overhaul would take a year and cost £750,000, but both estimates were wildly out.

THE FALSE DAWN

Following a protracted overhaul, 'reborn' *Flying Scotsman* was unveiled to the waiting world at the museum on the evening of May 27, 2011, in its former wartime black livery as NE No. 502.

However, all was not right.

The A4 boiler that had been carried by the A3 in its previous running days had been sold by the museum, which instead decided, for the sake of historical authenticity, to repair the spare A3 one, which was duly sent to Ian Riley's workshops at Bury.

However, issues arose with the boiler restoration, which pushed back the completion date, and then other major problems, including misaligned frames and a cracked right-hand cylinder, were discovered. A further public appeal was launched in a bid to raise £250,000 towards the repairs.

Within weeks of the high-profile relaunch, further defects were discovered, including numerous latent cracks throughout the frame assembly

Black-liveried *Flying Scotsman* undergoes test running at Bury Bolton Street station in East Lancashire Railway service on January 8, 2016. ROBIN JONES

as well as cracks in the horn blocks.

The main stretcher bar, horn ties and middle cylinder motion bracket were found to be beyond repair, and

new replacements were ordered. An independent report was commissioned, which reported the museum had vastly underestimated the work required because of the poor condition of the A3, partly down to a rushed inspection.

In October 2013, the museum announced Ian Riley had successfully tendered to complete the restoration, in return for being allowed to operate it for the first two years.

It was subsequently decided, for historical accuracy, to return the locomotive to service in the form it was withdrawn in 1963, numbered 60103, with double chimney, smoke deflectors and Brunswick green livery.

As such *Flying Scotsman* finally emerged from Riley's Baron Street works in Bury after dark on the evening on January 6, 2016. For the next two weekends, it underwent running-in trips on the adjoining East Lancashire Railway, seats on the trains selling out quickly as around 20,000 people arrived to see it back in action.

The crowds had never forgotten a real winner.

The unveiling of *Flying Scotsman* in wartime black livery as NE No. 502 in the Great Hall of the National Railway Museum at York on May 27, 2011. Sadly, a subsequent examination showed the locomotive was far from ready to run again. ROBIN JONES

MASS TRESPASS HALTS A NATIONAL TREASURE

Its unofficial main line comeback run, still in NE black, was the Railway Touring Company's 'Winter Cumbrian Mountain Express' from Carnforth to Carlisle on February 6.

However, a hot bearing and spring needed attention, and then a cracked driving wheel spring was discovered. The leading pair of driving wheels were removed and sent to Bury, where the bearings were examined and the problem rectified.

The wheels were refitted on February 19, and a test run from York to Scarborough completed on February 23.

No. 60103, by then repainted into Brunswick green livery, and a support

View from the sky: *Flying Scotsman* departs from King's Cross on February 25, 2016, with its official comeback tour on February 25, 2016. VIRGIN TRAINS

Crowds greet *Flying Scotsman* as it pulls into York station with its official comeback trip from King's Cross on February 25, 2016. It had arrived late after two instances of trespass on the East Coast Main Line caused by over-enthusiastic fans, ROBIN JONES

RIGHT: Penny Vaudoyer, daughter of *Flying Scotsman* saviour Alan Pegler, and Sir William McAlpine, who rescued the A3 from California, welcome the restored locomotive to the National Railway Museum on February 25. ROBIN JONES

coach ran down the East Coast Main Line to London on February 24, in time for its official comeback run from King's Cross to York the next morning.

Friday, February 25, 2016, saw *Flying Scotsman* haul its 11-coach train out of King's Cross at 7.40am. A total of 297 VIPs, fundraisers, competition winners and members of the public, who paid up to $450 each, were on board the relaunch trip. They included Davina Pike, who had been Alan Pegler's personal assistant on the tour of North America, and former owner Sir William McAlpine and his wife Judy. "It's a wonderful locomotive, like a beautiful woman," he said. "She's in the right place doing the right thing and very much loved by everybody, and the wonderful thing about her, she makes people smile, people love her."

Crowds not only gathered at the station and along the route....but on the track itself – a phenomenon that, sadly, would repeat itself in the years to come, including in the above-mentioned incident in Staffordshire on May 5, 2019.

At spots near St Neots and north of Doncaster, the locomotive was brought to a stop because of trespassers eager to get the closest view possible of No. 60103. Again, its celebrity status overrode any individual considerations of health and safety.

Trespass would become a big issue for the operator of the locomotive in the months that followed. When a subsequent planned trip through East Anglia was cancelled because of fears of trespass, it appeared the locomotive, which back in 1963 so nearly ended up as packs of razor blades, was now too famous to run.

However, the cost of $4.5m to overhaul the locomotive, a figure released by the museum in September 2016, over and above the $2.31m purchase price, not only made *Flying Scotsman* the most famous locomotive in the world, but the most expensive, too.

Yet all thoughts of the costly mistakes that had been made in the long-running overhaul quickly evaporated as far as a delighted and enthusiastic general public were concerned, with *Flying Scotsman* resuming its main line career.

Penny (then aged 17) with father Alan Pegler on *Flying Scotsman* during his period of the ownership of the locomotive. PENNY VAUDOYER

TWO POIGNANT FAREWELLS

Alan Pegler passed away on March 18, 2012, aged 91. On Saturday, October 13, 2018, tour operator Steam Dreams ran the King's Cross-York 'Alan Pegler Farewell' special – hauled by *Flying Scotsman* – at the request of Alan's daughter Penny Vaudoyer, enabling a request laid out in his will that half of his ashes would be placed in *Flying Scotsman's* firebox as the 4-6-2 was climbing Stoke Bank, the other half to be given similar treatment on the Ffestiniog Railway.

During the outward journey to York, and after the train had departed Peterborough, Penny was escorted onto 'Scotsman's' footplate, gaining access via the A3's tender corridor.

The committal of Alan's ashes was accompanied by a long blast on 'Scotsman's' whistle, passengers remaining silent as a mark of respect.

A second blast signalled the end

Flying Scotsman departs Bridgnorth station with a flourish on September 21, 2016, during the Severn Valley Railway's Pacific Power event. ROBIN JONES

No. 60103 *Flying Scotsman* leaves York station to move into the National Railway Museum's yard after heading the 'Scotsmans's Salute' to former owner Sir William McAlpine on January 11, 2019. NRM

of the minute's silence, inviting passengers to toast Alan's memory and achievements with a glass of champagne.

On Friday, January 11, 2019, the rail industry and the heritage sector joined forces to pay tribute to Sir William McAlpine, when a special memorial trip, the 'Scotsman's Salute', ran from King's Cross to York, again headed by *Flying Scotsman*. Sir William had died in hospital, aged 82, on March 4, 2018.

The landmark trip was organised by locomotive owner the National Railway Museum in partnership with East Coast franchise operator LNER, train operator DB Cargo, Riley & Son (E) Ltd, which operates the A3 on behalf of the museum, ticket sales handler UK Railtours, and Sir William's widow, Lady Judy McAlpine.

Tickets were also eagerly snapped up by members of the public at £159 each. In Sir William's memory, ticket sales will be used to fund an engineering training place for one young person, who will spend the year travelling around the country maintaining *Flying Scotsman*, and if they meet the standard at the end, will be offered a permanent job.

Following arrival at York and a break for lunch, passengers were invited to join members of the public at a naming ceremony for DB Class 90 electric No. 90028 on the turntable in the Great Hall. It was permanently named *Sir William McAlpine* in his honour.

At the ceremony, speakers praised Sir William for his contribution to railway preservation in glowing terms. However, perhaps the greatest accolade of all was the fact thousands of people turned out alongside the East Coast Main Line, despite it being a midweek working day, to glimpse or photograph *Flying Scotsman* in action, from stations, overbridges and every other vantage point.

Had it not been for Sir William, the locomotive would almost certainly have not been there, or might not even exist today.

NRM head of operations Jim Lowe said: "On behalf of myself, colleagues and volunteers I would like to publicly thank Sir William for his significant contribution to the museum and to the wider preservation of railway heritage in this country.

"Holding this memorial tour, naming a locomotive after him and especially setting up an engineering bursary to benefit young people, will create a fitting legacy to honour his memory."

Lady Judy McAlpine in front of the legendary locomotive that her late husband rescued from the United States, at the National Railway Museum, following the 'Scotsman's Salute' memorial train on January 11, 2019. ROBIN JONES

A LIVING LEGEND – OR AN ILLUSION?

During nearly a century in existence, *Flying Scotsman* has been greatly modified, altered or 'improved' since it first appeared from Doncaster works in 1922.

The question that is often asked is: How much of the locomotive as-built still exists?

Indeed, all that is left of the original of 1922/23 and the locomotive that reached 100mph in 1934 is the rear two thirds of the frames, part of the cab sides, some parts of the motion, and possibly the driving wheel splashers.

Tradition holds the frames of a locomotive give it an identity, and change as many other parts as you like, it will still be the locomotive as built. Yet in so many respects, the *Flying Scotsman* of today is more of an historical entity than a physical artefact in its own right.

Some may even argue it is on the verge of being a new-build locomotive, a replica in its own right.

Yet, as we said on the Isle of Purbeck in March 2019, the public have long since taken the greatest locomotive legend of them all to their hearts.

That seem very unlikely to change.

Chapter 8

Royal Scot:

THE 'IMPOSTER' THAT WOWED AMERICA

BELOW: LMS 4-6-0 No. 46100 *Royal Scot* passes Conway Castle with Saphos Trains' 'North Wales Coast Express' from Crewe to Holyhead on April 14, 2018. ROBERT FALCONER

M IS FOR MIDLAND
WITH ENGINES GALORE
TWO ON EACH TRAIN
AND ASKING FOR MORE

So ran the satirical rhyme about the Midland Railway's infamous small engine policy, which meant whenever it had to run express trains over the West Coast Main Line, it had to 'double up' – two engines and twice the number of footplate crews.

Such trains were hauled by pairs of Midland Compound 4-4-0s between Glasgow and Carnforth, and a LNWR Claughton 4-6-0, piloted by an LNWR George V 4-4-0, southwards to Euston.

The net result was more and shorter trains had to be run, while paths had to be created for locomotives running light engine back to base after double heading or banking duties.

However, all that was to eventually change in the wake of the creation of Britain's 'Big Four' companies after the Grouping in 1923, or passing of The Railways Act 1921.

At the outbreak of the First World War, there were around 120 railway companies in the UK. Many of them duplicated services and routes offered by their rivals, with the result that both made losses.

During the war, the nation's railways came under state control, for strategic and economic reasons. For the duration of the conflict, much of the needless rivalry ended, when Britain's railways were run for the general good of the country rather than shareholders of individual companies.

In response to post-war calls to nationalise the entire railway network, the government of David Lloyd George opted for a 'halfway house' measure by which most of them were grouped into four big companies: the Great Western Railway, the Southern Railway, the London & North Eastern Railway and the London Midland & Scottish Railway.

Prior to the enforced merger, the London & North Western Railway merged with the Lancashire & Yorkshire Railway from January 1, 1922, bringing together 2667 route miles. The pair then became the biggest constituent of the LMS, which also absorbed the Caledonian Railway, the Furness Railway, the Glasgow & South Western Railway, the Highland Railway, the North Staffordshire Railway, three companies in Northern Ireland – the Dundalk, Newry & Greenore Railway, the Northern Counties Committee, the Joint Midland & Great Northern of Ireland Railway – and the LNWR's old rival, the Midland Railway.

The LMS became the world's biggest transport organisation overnight, the

Midland Compound 4-4-0 No. 1000, part of the National Collection, on display inside Barrow Hill roundhouse, near Chesterfield, on September 26, 2015. ROBIN JONES

largest commercial undertaking in the British Empire, and UK's second largest employer after the Post Office. It also claimed to be the largest joint stock organisation in the world.

However, the early years of the LMS were plagued by infighting between the two old enemies, the LNWR and the Midland, as they competed for control of the new company.

The higher management of the LMS became led by Midland men, who were set to prove Derby ways were the best, and managed to have the Midland's Crimson Lake livery adopted as standard by the LMS.

However, the former Crewe and Derby regimes could not agree over locomotives.

Crewe had followed a 'raw power' approach, with powerful locomotives turned out to take heavy loads over long distances, such as the West Coast Main Line – a dramatic contrast to the Midland's 'little engine' policy, with

The left-hand nameplate of No. 6100 *Royal Scot*, which was fixed to the locomotive after its historic tour of North America and is still carried by the locomotive today. HUGH LLEWELLYN*

smart, polished, immaculately turned out but smaller locomotives, which often double-headed even modest loading.

The origin of this culture clash lay in the fact the LNWR had been built to tackle hilly and mountainous country north of Manchester, while George Stephenson had engineered the Midland main lines with shallow gradients, for which smaller engines were adequate for most occasions.

Yet when the Settle to Carlisle route was opened, the small Midland engines were inadequate on their own, and the Midland by necessity resorted to double heading or banking.

However, the Midland had declined to introduce types like the LNWR's successful 4-6-0s for express passenger trains and adhered to its stock-in-trade 4-4-0 designs. The net result was the newly formed LMS found itself desperately short of big locomotives. While the Midland compounds could handle the Euston to Birmingham New Street expresses, they were unsuitable for the Anglo-Scottish trains.

In the summer of 1927, the LMS introduced the new prestige 'Royal Scot' train from Euston to Glasgow. The 15-coach train needed to be hauled by an LNWR Claughton, assisted by a George the Fifth or Precursor, south of Carnforth, and taken by a pair of new compounds over Shap Summit. But…if only one locomotive could do the whole job…

LMS chief mechanical engineer

GWR 4-6-0 No. 5000 *Launceston Castle*, the locomotive that changed LMS thinking, as portrayed in an official GWR works photograph.

George Hughes retired in 1925 and was replaced by Sir Henry Fowler, who has held the same position with the Midland. It was Fowler and another former Midland mechanical engineer, James Edward Anderson, who had been responsible for the badly lacking small-engine policy the LMS had adopted.

However, Fowler decided to tackle the West Coast traction shortcomings, and in 1926 began designing a compound Pacific express locomotive – only for the LMS management to disapprove.

In a bid to solve an impasse that resulted from this disagreement, the LMS borrowed the Great Western Railway's 4-6-0 No. 5000 *Launceston Castle* for a month, testing it between Euston and Carlisle. The Castles, GWR chief mechanical engineer Charles Collett's development of George Jackson Churchward's Star class of 1907, were hugely successful from the start and set exacting new standards everywhere.

Launceston Castle impressed the LMS management to the extent it asked the GWR to build a batch of Castles for the railway, only to be met with a blanket refusal, as it did when it also asked to borrow a set to Castle drawings. The LMS board cancelled Fowler's Pacific project, and replaced it with a 4-6-0 with three cylinders and a simple-expansion steam circuit, which was dubbed as an 'Improved Castle'.

The LMS commissioned the North British Locomotive Company of Glasgow to build 50 of these engines within a year because of inherited inadequacies at both Crewe and Derby works.

Derby's drawing office, under chief draughtsman Herbert Chambers, worked alongside North British staff in designing the class, with the help of a set of drawings of the Southern Railway's Lord Nelson 4-6-0s, which provided the firebox design.

Derby practice was still followed in that the cylinders and valve gear were derived from Fowler's 2-6-4T, which was being designed at former Midland works at the same time. The end product was the Royal Scot class of 4-6-0s, at first named after British army regiments and, until 1935/36, famous LNWR locomotives. North British received the contract in December 1926 and the first Royal Scot was delivered seven months later. A further 20 were built by Derby Works.

Southern Railway 4-6-0 E850 *Lord Nelson* on the Mid-Hants Railway. Features of this class contributed to the design of the Royal Scots. ROBIN JONES

No. 6100 *Royal Scot* on the Canadian leg of its tour in November 1933. NRM

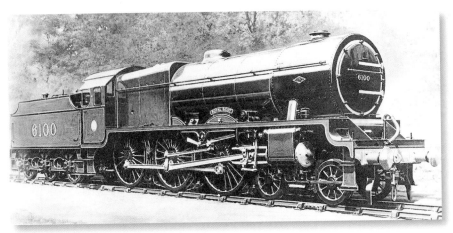

A 1927 LMS postcard view of the first of the *Royal Scot* 4-6-0s – No. 6100 *Royal Scot*, as outshopped in 1927. This locomotive later changed identities with sister No. 6152 *The Kings Dragoon Guardsman*.

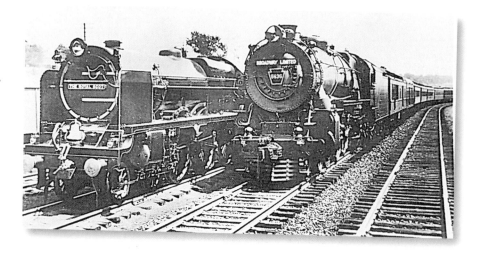

THE ROYAL SCOT DELIVERS THE GOODS!

In October 1927 the first Royal Scots were delivered to the LMS, revolutionising services on the West Coast from London to Manchester, Carlisle and Glasgow. The design turned out to be a classic, capable of hauling 420-ton trains unaided over Shap and Beattock.

The Royal Scots were immediately assigned to the top LMS expresses, smoke deflectors being added after 1931 to prevent the driver's vision from being obscured.

One class member was sent across the Atlantic to attend the Century of Progress Exhibition in Chicago in 1933, and to undertake a series of runs in both the US and Canada, covering 11,194 miles, travelling from Montreal to Missouri, and even crossing the Rocky Mountains.

It was inspected by more than three million people. The aim was to demonstrate the progress and development which had taken place in British passenger train construction.

The theme of the fair was technological innovation, with the motto Science Finds, Industry Applies, Man

LEFT: *Royal Scot* joins crack US train the 'Broadway Limited' for the 1933 tour of North America.

Adapts. One description of the fair noted that the world, "then still mired in the malaise of the Great Depression, could glimpse a happier not-too-distant future, all driven by innovation in science and technology". The exhibition "emphasized technology and progress, a utopia, or perfect world, founded on democracy and manufacturing".

For the transatlantic visit, a Royal Scot class member that was due for general overhaul was chosen, in this case No. 6152 *The Kings Dragoon Guardsman*. The coupled axleboxes were replaced with larger ones, based on a GWR design, and the bogie replaced by a De Glehn type, also derived from GWR practice.

No. 6152 assumed the identity of the first member of the class, No. 6100, and kept the identity after returning to Britain, carrying an enlarged nameplate with details of its appearance at the exhibition, and therefore, as far as the identity of No. 6100 is concerned, might be regarded as an impostor!

The LMS rebuilt two LMS Jubilee 4-6-0s with Type 2A boilers in 1942, but later turned to the parallel-boilered Royal Scots, whose boilers and cylinders were life-expired, and whose smokeboxes were difficult to keep airtight. Between 1943 and 1955 the whole class was rebuilt to create the LMS Rebuilt Royal Scot type. These extensive rebuilds included new boilers, frames and cylinders, but in most cases the original frame stretchers, wheels, cab and fittings were retained.

As each locomotive arrived for rebuilding, it was stripped and the identity transferred to a fresh frameset prepared using the parts recovered from the locomotive that had previously been rebuilt. The new frames were slightly shorter than the originals.

Most rebuilt examples retained their own cab and wheels, but the frame stretchers, and other integral parts of the frame were from the previously rebuilt locomotives.

A derivate of the Royal Scot class were the Patriot or 'Baby Scot' class of 4-6-0s. They combined the chassis of the Royal Scot with the boiler from the LNWR Claughtons that had been rebuilt with bigger and more successful boilers. They too were an overnight success, and eventually 52 were constructed.

Many Patriots were later rebuilt, and all were withdrawn between 1960-65 and scrapped.

However, a project to build a full-size replica was launched in 2007 by the LMS-Patriot Project.

It will carry the number 45551 after the last built, and will be named *The Unknown Warrior*.

Heritage Railway magazine readers contributed £60,000 for the six driving wheels to be cast, and the project has continued to make steady progress.

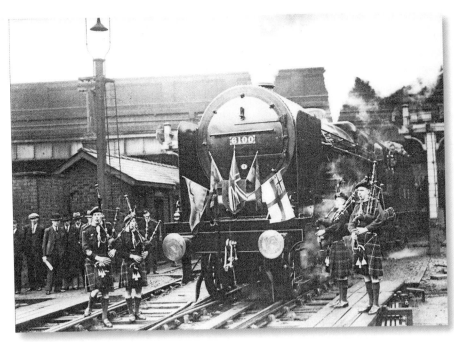

A LMS publicity picture of No. 6100 *Royal Scot*, or rather the locomotive that carried that identity from new, leaving Euston to Glasgow to promote its fast express services between Euston and Glasgow. The timetabled service first ran in 1862 and was eventually known as the 'Royal Scot'. ROBIN JONES COLLECTION

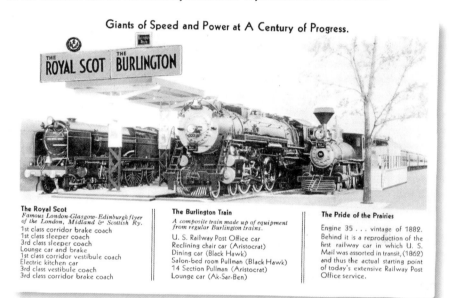

A brochure page comparing *Royal Scot* with giants of American railroads at the 1933 Century of Progress International Exposition.

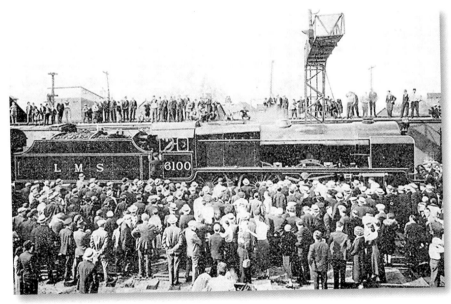

Royal Scot proved to be a major crowd puller during its 1933 transatlantic tour.

LEFT: LMS 4-6-0 No. 6100 *Royal Scot* in full flight, as depicted in a contemporary postcard. Note the lack of headboards, as the class was originally designed. ROBIN JONES COLLECTION

The cover of a souvenir booklet produced for the Century of Progress International Exposition in Chicago in 1933.

LEFT: A 1930s view of No. 6100 *Royal Scot* passing Leighton Buzzard. ROBIN JONES COLLECTION

NATIONALISATION AND WITHDRAWAL

After Nationalisation on January 1, 1948, No. 6100 was renumbered 46100, and two years later was rebuilt with a 2A taper boiler, and the words "Prior to conversion" were added to its nameplates. As such, it became a markedly different engine.

In October 1962, 46100 was withdrawn from service, in Nottingham.

At the time, Billy Butlin was buying redundant locomotives out of BR service and using them as attractions at his holiday camps, on static display, as objects of interest for younger visitors.

After cosmetic restoration into its original LMS crimson lake at Crewe Works (although *Royal Scot* never carried it after being rebuilt), it was towed from Crewe Works to Nottingham by LMS 'Black Five' No. 45038 and then onwards to Boston by B1 No. 61177 on June 12, 1963.

After a few days at Boston shed, No. 6100 was taken to Skegness behind an Ivatt 4MT. After three weeks in the goods yard there, it was taken by a Pickford's low loader for the short road trip to Butlin's Skegness camp at Ingoldmells. When it arrived there on July 18, 1963, it was appropriately welcomed by pipers from the 1st Battalion, The Royal Scots.

Once its class set records for the run from Euston to Glasgow: by the 1970s, No. 6100 *Royal Scot* was relegated to slow-speed trips on a short length of demonstration track at Bressingham Steam Museum in Norfolk. ROBIN JONES COLLECTION

Royal Scot became one of two class members preserved, the other being No. 6152 *Scots Guardsman*, all others having been withdrawn between 1962-65 and scrapped.

No. 6100 was plinthed at Skegness and remained there until the early-1970s, when it was acquired by the late horticulturalist Alan Bloom, founder of Bressingham Steam Museum, near

Diss, in Norfolk. March 16, 1971 saw No. 6100 departing from Skegness for Bressingham, where it returned to steam in 1972, being given demonstration runs on a short length of standard gauge track.

It ran until 1978 when it once more became a static exhibit. The Butlins empire completed its sale to Bressingham in May 1989.

THE RETURN TO STEAM

By the turn of the 21st century, Bressingham Steam Museum began seeking grant aid to return No. 6100 *Royal Scot* to the main line. Its trustees gave the go-ahead for the overhaul to be undertaken at Southall, under the auspices of then *Flying Scotsman* engineer Roland Kennington.

However, the original estimated cost of £306,000 rose to nearly £1million, with £429,000 being met by the Heritage Lottery Fund, with the overhaul taking five years to complete.

Then there were murmurings of discontent and disagreement about the chosen livery of LMS crimson lake, correct for the pre-Nationalisation number of 6100, but not for the post-Nationalisation taper boiler, which the locomotive now carried. This furore also brought into play the issue of smoke deflectors: 'To fit them or not', that was the question.

When the restoration finishing line was in sight and the planned return on the near horizon, the Bressingham trustees decided to move the overhaul away from the team at Southall and to music producer and locomotive enthusiast Pete Waterman's LNWR workshops at Crewe Heritage Centre.

Eventually, *Royal Scot* was poised to make its long and eagerly awaited comeback in steam. However, a near disaster struck on March 21, 2009, when *Royal Scot* caught fire while being transported by a large haulage specialist Allelys low loader down the M5.

A puncture caused a tyre on the low loader to catch fire beneath the locomotive between junctions 21 and 22, about 35 miles from its destination. It had been on its way to the March 26-29 spring steam gala at the West Somerset Railway.

Fortunately, the driver was close to Sedgemoor services, near Burnham-on-Sea, and he managed to pull onto the hard shoulder of the approach road. As the trailer caught fire, the tractor unit was immediately unhitched and, with the fire gaining hold, was driven into the service area.

Firemen from Weston-super-Mare and Burnham-on-Sea extinguished the blaze as police closed two lanes of the M5 while the fire was being tackled.

The damaged trailer, with *Royal Scot* aboard, remained on the hard shoulder leading to the service area, awaiting the arrival of a replacement. However, a successful loaded test run led to the locomotive taking its place in the gala timetable after all.

Controversy flared again when No. 6100 appeared at the Llangollen Railway Steam Steel & Stars II gala on April 18-26, 2019, minus the BR-style curved smoke deflectors, which had been carried on its return from restoration at the West Somerset Railway three weeks earlier. Pete Waterman said the LNWR Heritage workshops in Crewe was 'calling the shots' on whether they were fitted or not.

LMS 4-6-0 No. 36100 *Royal Scot* in light steam at Crewe on August 5, 2015. The cover for the air pump, which fits in the gap on the left-hand smoke deflector, hiding the pump from view, was still being manufactured when this picture was taken. PETER GREENWOOD

No. 46100 is seen passing Foxcovert Road footbridge, just north of Peterborough, on the route to Spalding, hauling the 1Z46 'The Lindum Fayre' annual tour from King's Cross to Lincoln for the Christmas market, which it had taken over at Peterborough on December 9, 2017. ALAN WILSON*

BACK ON THE MAIN LINE 50 YEARS ON

Following the fire mishap on the M5, the cost in time and resources of sending No. 6100 to the galas at Minehead and Llangollen, and the level of expertise needed to ready it for running on the main line, Bressingham Steam Museum started talks with potential investors about the future ownership of *Royal Scot*.

Eventually, the locomotive was acquired by the Royal Scot Locomotive and General Trust, a new charitable group overseen by multi-millionaire locomotive owner Jeremy Hosking. His trust later also bought Pete Waterman's LNWR heritage steam workshops. There, *Royal Scot* was given a full overhaul to modern main line standards.

In July 2015, *Royal Scot* has emerged from Crewe Heritage Centre sporting a coat of fresh BR Brunswick green paint, still lacking numbers or lining, but clearly close to steaming.

As No. 46100, *Royal Scot* arrived on the Severn Valley Railway and began a programme of test running on Wednesday, September 9, 2015, in readiness for the line's September 17-20 autumn steam gala.

It began its test by running light engine for three days, and a few items needing attention were highlighted. *Royal Scot* hauled it first public train for

LEFT: *Royal Scot* is not only a hugely popular performer on the 21st century main line but also a major crowd puller at heritage lines. Here, it is seen in action on the North Yorkshire Moors Railway on April 2, 2017, during a week of special services on the line. A major success for the NYMR, the visit generated a surplus approaching a six-figure sum. CHARLIE JACKSON*

more than six years at the gala.

After returning from the gala, *Royal Scot* and its support coach departed Crewe on Monday, December 21 for an overnight stop at Carnforth in preparation for its loaded test run the following morning.

Departing Carnforth, the trip was routed via Settle Junction, Hellifield, Clitheroe, Blackburn, Preston and Lancaster, before returning. Then as planned, the engine and coach set off back to Crewe via Preston, Wigan North West and Warrington Bank Quay, arriving just before midnight. It was its first loaded main line train in more than 50 years.

The proving run was a success, and so *Royal Scot* made its public main line passenger-carrying debut on Saturday, February 6, 2016, working Railway Touring Company's 'North Wales Coast Express' between Crewe, Chester and Holyhead and return. *Royal Scot* was back.

There followed a plethora of bookings that kept the 4-6-0 busy on the national network.

It was hired to work the Bristol to Grange-over-Sands leg of the Railway Touring company's 'Great Britain IX' tour on April 28, and made a second trip to Holyhead on May 28, working Pathfinder Tours' 'Yns Mon Express' from Swindon, steam coming on at Crewe.

Royal Scot threads its way through Teignmouth with the Down leg of the Railway Touring Company's 'Great Britain' railtour on April 26, 2016. BARRY LEWIS*

Working out of Bristol Temple Meads, *Royal Scot* was booked to head the 'Torbay Express' to Paignton and Kingswear for the first part of the train's summer programme.

It was the first time that a 'Scot' had worked west of Bristol since the BR Locomotive Exchanges in 1948.

During a visit to Scotland, *Royal Scot* travelled over the Forth Bridge on some spectacular journeys from Edinburgh along the shores of the Firth of Forth.

So, after an absence of more than half a century, *Royal Scot* is back on the national network with a vengeance.

David Ward, who retired from a 45-year BR career in 1994 as director, special trains, underlined the locomotive's legendary status when he described No. 6100 as "generally regarded as the best 4-6-0 to run on BR main lines".

Resplendent in LMS crimson lake, but without those BR era smoke deflectors: No. 6100 *Royal Scot* heads west to Carrog on the Llangollen Railway on April 19, 2009. ROBIN JONES

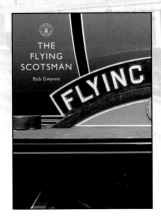 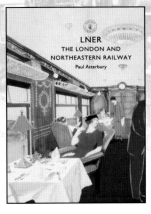  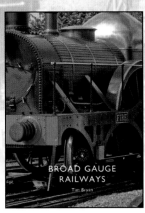

Chapter 9

The legend that is 'Lizzie':

PRINCESS OF THE WEST COAST

When William Stanier was asked to provide faster and more powerful locomotives for the West Coast route from London to Glasgow, he excelled at the challenge, and in 1936 one of his first LMS Pacifics set a set world record in the process, immortalising Princess Royal No. 6201 *Princess Elizabeth* in legend – one which is still very much alive today.

TOP: No. 6201 *Princess Elizabeth* passing Clitheroe Castle en route from Carnforth to Blackburn on its loaded test run on March 28, 2019. BRIAN DOBBS

RIGHT: LMS chief mechanical engineer Sir William Stanier, who designed, among others, the Princess Royal class, the first Pacifics for the railway.

When Sir William Stanier was appointed as chief mechanical engineer of the LMS, the 'Big Four' company did not possess a single locomotive that could take a 500-ton express by itself for all of the 401 miles from Euston to Glasgow.

The inherited Midland Railway 'small engines' policy was now history, and the company told Stanier to rectify the issue without delay.

He duly ordered the building of three prototype Pacifics, the first of which, No. 6200 *The Princess Royal*, was completed on June 27, 1933.

It was derived to a large extent from the GWR King 4-6-0, reflecting Stanier's previous and long career with the Swindon empire.

Basically, the new locomotive was for all intents and purposes a King with a larger firebox, supported by additional trailing wheels.

The success of No. 2700 led to two batches being built.

The engines were named after princesses. The official name for the class was selected because Mary, the Princess Royal, was the Commander-in-Chief of the Royal Scots

The first batch of two included the second example, No. 6201 *Princess Elizabeth*.

It was built in November 1933 at Crewe Works and named after the seven-year-old future Queen Elizabeth II, elder daughter of Albert, Duke of York, later King George VI.

Despite the class officially being named after No. 6200 *Princess Royal*, they became nicknamed "Lizzies" after 6201.

A second batch of 11 was built,

including a single example of a version using non-condensing steam turbines instead of cylinders. However, this locomotive, No. 6202, was in a separate class of its own, known as the Turbomotive, and was later rebuilt in conventional form in 1952 and named *Princess Anne*, but was destroyed in the Harrow & Wealdstone disaster later that year.

The class was assigned to head the 'Royal Scot' train between Euston and Glasgow, replacing the Royal Scot 4-6-0s.

At the time, it was nearly four decades since the last late-Victorian 'Race to the North' between the companies operating the rival East and West Coast main lines, and the Preston fatal crash of 1896, which overnight turned public opinion firmly against 'racing' and speeding trains.

Yet by the Thirties, times had changed: the UK was battling its way out of the gloom of a recession as best it might, and the 'Big Four' companies needed to boost their revenues, especially from the long-haul expresses like the London to Scotland routes.

The old agreements about adherence to speed limits were shelved, and racing to the north of the border was not only back on but pursued with a vengeance far greater than ever before.

The LNER had launched the famous non-stop 'Flying Scotsman' express from London to Edinburgh in 1927, using special tenders with corridors, which allowed engine crew changes at speed.

However, the rival LMS had the Royal Scot, which was more than capable of responding. It ran its own non-stop trains from London to Glasgow behind a Royal Scot, and used a standard Compound 4-4-0 to complete the 399-mile London to Edinburgh run.

In 1933, the launch of the 'Flying Hamburger' high-speed diesel railcar in Germany made worldwide headlines. At first it appeared the steam age was over – but diesels and electrics would have to wait decades to have it all their own way.

The fastest train in Britain in the early-1930s was the GWR's 'Cheltenham Spa Express', known unofficially as the 'Cheltenham Flyer', for which Castles averaged 71.3mph between Swindon and Paddington.

LNER chief mechanical engineer Nigel Gresley set out to introduce a long-distance, high-speed train service on the East Coast Main Line in 1935.

On November 30, 1934, Gresley's 4-6-2 No. 4472 *Flying Scotsman* reached 100mph, the first steam locomotive in the world officially to do so, on Stoke Bank in Lincolnshire, during a test run between Leeds and King's Cross. On the outward trip to Leeds, with renowned driver William Sparshatt in charge, No. 4472 had taken four coaches 185.8

Princess Royal 4-6-2 No. 6201 *Princess Elizabeth* carrying the famous 703 headcode as it undertakes a record London to Glasgow run on November 16, 1936.

miles from King's Cross to Leeds in 151 minutes six seconds.

Forgetting the reservations described earlier that were held by the GWR about revealing *City of Truro's* unofficial 102.3mph in 1904, the LNER pulled no punches in making maximum publicity from the feat.

In March 1935, again with driver Sparshatt at the regulator, A3 No. 2750 *Papyrus* ran from King's Cross to Newcastle and back with six coaches. The 500 miles were covered in 423 minutes 23 seconds, including 300 miles at 80mph average, and reaching 108mph at one point – setting a new world record.

These feats led to the building of the A4 Pacifics, Gresley's streamlined development of the A1s/A3s.

The engines were designed to work the 'Silver Jubilee', covering the 232.3 miles from Darlington to King's Cross at an average of 70.4mph, only slightly slower than the GWR train, but over more than twice the distance. On the press demonstration run of September 27, 1935, the new Gresley A4 No. 2509 *Silver Link* twice hit 112mph, taking the world record away from *Papyrus*.

The LNER's second streamlined train, the 'Coronation', took the King's Cross to Edinburgh time down to six hours, just about beating the scheduled non-stop average speed of the 'Cheltenham Flyer'.

The LMS knew it could not sit back and watch, and so Stanier had to come up with a fresh formula… and fast.

Driver Tom Clark is congratulated by LMS officials after bringing *Princess Elizabeth* into Glasgow Central station from Euston at 3.43pm on November 16, 1936, setting a new world record, with an average speed of 68.2mph.

'LIZZIE'S FIRST FINEST HOUR

The LMS drew up a potential schedule for a six-hour non-stop service from Euston to Glasgow. However, a trial run had to be first carried out to see if such a plan was feasible.

Tom Clark, the senior driver from 5A Crewe North shed, from where loco-men worked south to London and north to Perth, was selected for this vital test trip.

Clark, who had joined the LNWR in December 1888 and worked through the links from cleaner to driver, would be assisted by fireman Charles Fleet and passed fireman Albert Shaw, on what would bring him overnight fame.

The test train was designated 703, and No. 6201 *Princess Elizabeth* was selected to haul it.

Clark and his crew – the '5A Three' – went to London the night before the special runs, lodging with other engine men in the noisy and 'not-select-in-any-way' railwaymen's 'barracks' at Camden shed.

On November 16, 1936, Clark and his crew drove the train from London to Glasgow in five hours 53 minutes 38 seconds – and showed the LMS was easily a match for Gresley and the LNER.

The following day, Clark and his crew completed the return journey in five

Vintage Wills cigarettes collectors' card depicting No. 6201 *Princess Elizabeth*.

hours 44 minutes 14 seconds. Glasgow Central to Euston non-stop had been achieved at an average speed of 69mph, with an average load of 240 tons.

The three were instantly hailed as national heroes, and when they arrived back at Euston, they were taken to Broadcasting House and interviewed by the BBC.

National newspapers splashed with front-page headlines proclaiming '401 Miles Non Stop", "Railway Ambition Achieved", and "London-Glasgow Under 6 Hours".

Thanks to the '5A Three', Stanier and the LMS directors knew they had made

the right decision with their plans for the soon-to-be-unveiled 'Coronation Scot' service.

As a result, Hornby, the Liverpool manufacturer of model railways, produced an O-gauge model of No. 6201. When it was launched on May 1, 1937, Hornby arranged for a photograph to be staged at Edge Hill depot, Liverpool, with two schoolboys holding a model alongside the full-size locomotive with Clark and Fleet. Clark was reported as having said "it's grand", a well-known phrase of the day.

On July 12, 1937, Clark drove the Royal Train from Crewe to Euston. On reaching the terminus, King George VI, who had been travelling with Queen Elizabeth, Princess Elizabeth and Princess Margaret, summoned Tom from the footplate.

Unwashed and still wearing his overalls, the King conferred on him the OBE for his record runs to and from Glasgow in 1936.

Tom retired in 1938 and continued to live in Crewe, pursuing his interests in fishing and snooker. He died aged 80 in January 1954, after a short illness.

During its working career for the LMS, No. 6201 carried the famous LMS

A pre-war postcard view of the 1936 Euston to Glasgow record-breaker. ROBIN JONES COLLECTION

The ill-fated Turbomotive pictured after rebuilding in 1952. NRM

No. 6201 *Princess Elizabeth* with the 'Scarborough Flyer' at Wakefield Kirkgate on August 7, 2009. DAVID SPENCER*

Crimson Lake livery, and at one stage, LMS black. After Nationalisation in 1948, BR renumbered *Princess Elizabeth* as 46201. During its time with the nationalised railway, it carried both BR Brunswick green and BR black, both of which were lined out.

With the onset of dieselisation in the wake of BR's 1955 Modernisation Plan, and the delivery of increasing numbers of Type 4 2000hp locomotives, No. 6201 was placed in store in March 1961.

However, failures of the new diesels were commonplace, and to maintain services, No. 6201 was returned to traffic in May 1961.

But with the available diesel fleet having once again been bolstered, that October, No. 6021 was again placed into storage at Carlisle Kingmoor – only to be returned to service in January 1962 because of yet more diesel non-availabilities.

It was returned to traffic to cover for diesel failures and continued to work until September 1962 where it was once again placed into storage. It was subsequently withdrawn by BR in October 1962 and bought by Roger Bell straight out of service.

The Princess Elizabeth Locomotive Society was born, to ensure a living legend did not end up at the mercy of the scrapman, like so many other legendary locomotives both before it and afterwards.

The Hornby advertisement showing two schoolboys from Liverpool (where Meccano/ Hornby were based) receiving a scale model of No. 6201 *Princess Elizabeth* from 1936 record-run driver and firemen Tom Clark and Charles Fleet in 1937.

Princess Elizabeth in Settle and Carlisle action on the approach to Ribblehead with the Railway Touring Company's northbound 'The Hadrian' special on April 17, 2010. BRIAN DOBBS

No. 6201 leaving Llandudno station in August 2010 with the Railway Touring Company's 'North Wales Coast Express' return excursion to Liverpool Lime Street. BRIAN DOBBS

A STARRING ROLE IN ITS SECOND LIFE

No. 6021 was first kept at the former Dowty Railway Preservation Society's premises at Ashchurch, in Gloucestershire, and then moved to the Bulmers Railway Centre at the cider manufacturer's plant in Hereford.

At the end of main line steam haulage in August 1968, British Railways banned all steam locomotives from the national network – the exception being the 1ft 11½in-gauge Vale of Rheidol Railway, which was then still in public ownership.

The BR steam ban was released after GWR 4-6-0 No. 5000 *King George V* made a ban-breaking run with the Bulmers Cider Train in October 1971, and the following year, a select number of preserved locomotives were allowed to run tours on the main line.

Princess Elizabeth made its comeback to the national network in 1976. On April 24 that year, it headed two specials: 'The Gwentman', from Shrewsbury via Newport to Hereford, and the 'Intercity', from Hereford to Chester, both as part of longer tours involving Bulleid Merchant Navy Pacific No. 35028 *Clan Line*.

Fittingly, *Princess Elizabeth* worked the 'Stanier Centenary' on June 5, 1976, marking the 100th birthday of its designer, who was born on May 27, 1876. In the years following its comeback, *Princess Elizabeth* became one of the most popular performers in the heritage steam era.

The Bulmers Centre closed in 1993, and No. 6201 moved to what is now the Midland Railway-Butterley in Derbyshire. An overhaul of the locomotive and tender was started there, but with most work spread between both Tyseley Locomotive works in Birmingham and Bury, the locomotive was not completed until 2002.

No. 6201 was briefly based in 2009 at Crewe Heritage Centre in 2009.

Over the weekend of November 12/13, 2011, No. 6201 *Princess Elizabeth* proudly marked the 75th anniversary of one of the most celebrated runs in British locomotive history, that epic 1936 non-stop run between Euston and Glasgow, and back again. From Crewe, it headed the Vintage Trains 10-coach 'Coronation Scot' on the 243-mile run to Glasgow, calling only at Carlisle for servicing and a crew change. It ran the next 101 miles non-stop via Beattock to Glasgow, carrying an exact replica of the special '703' headboard worn on the original run, which was not named.

No. 6201 was withdrawn from service in July 2012 for a piston and valve examination at Tyseley, and following repairs it returned to service

LMS Princess Royal No. 6201 *Princess Elizabeth* signalling the start of the Diamond Jubilee Thames pageant by sounding its whistle from Battersea Railway Bridge on June 3, 2012. CHRISBWAH*

that November heading the 'Cumbrian Mountaineer' for Vintage Trains, from Carnforth to Crewe via Shap Summit, returning via the Settle and Carlisle line to Crewe, from where a diesel returned the special to Tyseley.

The Diamond Jubilee year of Queen Elizabeth II came in 2012. June 3 saw No. 6201 arrive in London with a Vintage Trains tour from Tyseley. While standing on Battersea Railway Bridge, No. 6201's whistle signalled the start of the Thames Diamond Jubilee Pageant, a parade of 670 boats on the Tideway of the Thames.

The Queen, Prince Philip and other members of the Royal Family were aboard vessels that took part in the parade, organised by the Thames Diamond Jubilee Foundation, and funded by private donations and sponsorship.

According to Guinness World Records, it was the largest parade of boats ever assembled, beating the previous record of 327 vessels, set in Bremerhaven, Germany, in 2011. Taking part were military, commercial and pleasure craft. Her Majesty was aware of the locomotive and waved to the crew on the footplate.

Five weeks later, on July 11, No. 6201 hauled the Royal Train from Newport to Hereford and again from Worcester to Oxford as part of the Diamond Jubilee Tour. The locomotive carried the traditional four-lamp combination (one lamp at the top of the smokebox and three on the buffer lamp irons) used on trains conveying the head of state.

It was only the second time in the

Seen from Clapham Moor, No. 6201 *Princess Elizabeth* undertakes its loaded test run from Carnforth and back on March 28, 2019. ANDREW*

preservation era the Queen had been conveyed on a steam-hauled Royal Train on the main line: the previous occasion came in No. 2002 when Princess Coronation Pacific No. 2002 *Duchess of Sutherland* performed the honour – with No. 6201 as standby engine.

The July 11 trip came just a few weeks before the 50th anniversary of the purchase of the locomotive, which has been owned by the Princess Elizabeth Locomotive Society longer than under both the LMS and BR.

No. 6201 was withdrawn for overhaul at the end of December 2012, having completed its longest period of operation in preservation.

It returned to steam in June 2015 after a heavy overhaul and was featured in Tyseley's June 27-28 open weekend, but did not return to main line service until the following year, when it was based

at Southall depot in London to work railtours in southern England.

Its comeback happened on August 23 that year, when it hauled Steam Dreams' 'Cathedrals Express' from London Victoria via Taunton and the West Somerset Railway to Minehead and back.

The locomotive proceeded to generate even more headlines by visiting parts of the country where no other LMS Princess Royal had been before, such as Norwich, Penzance and Swanage.

However, it was later withdrawn from service in late 2016 because of multiple problems being found with the locomotive's boiler.

Repairs were carried out at the Princess Royal Class Locomotive Trust's West Shed at the Midland Railway-Butterley, home of the second surviving class member, No. 46203 *Princess*

Margaret Rose, hence the name of that society. February 22, 2018 saw 'Lizzie' move to West Coast Railways' Carnforth depot for boiler repairs and other general maintenance, behind two West Coast Railways Class 37 diesels.

No. 6201 and its support coach underwent a test run from Carnforth to Hellifield on March 14, 2019. This threw up minor snags which were rectified in time for a second loaded test run around the Carnforth proving circuit on March 28, taking five BR Mk1 coaches via Blackburn and Preston.

* New members are always welcome in the Princess Elizabeth Locomotive Society. Membership costs just £20 per year, £15 for those 60 and over, juniors £10. For more details visit 6201.co.uk or write to the membership secretary, 112 Draycott Road, Upper Tean ST10 4JF.

No. 6201 heads 'The Cumbrian Mountaineer' across
Birkbeck Viaduct on November 17, 2002.*

Chapter 10

The fastest

Britain invented the steam railway locomotive, and on Sunday, July 3, 1938, took it to unsurpassed heights when LNER A4 Pacific No. 4468 reached **126mph** on Stoke Bank in Lincolnshire.

LNER streamlined A4 Pacific No. 4468 *Mallard* pictured on September 8, 2013, as part of celebrations to mark the 75th anniversary of its world record run down Stoke Bank. It was displayed on a newly laid sidings in the yard at Grantham station, a few miles to the north. ROBIN JONES

LEGEND OF THEM ALL

Nº 4468

A4

When Sir Nigel Gresley, in his capacity as LNER chief mechanical engineer, asked his technical assistant Norman Newsome to arrange a set of carriages for a brake test on the East Coast Main Line, the request would normally have seemed nothing out of the ordinary.

However, Newsome had earlier been told Gresley hoped to beat the 114mph UK record set by the LMS with Stanier's Princess Coronation Pacific No. 6220 *Coronation*.

Not only that, but Gresley and the LNER had become concerned about developments in rail travel technology in Nazi Germany. He had already looked at the 'Flying Hamburger' high-speed diesel railcar set, which ran for long stretches at 85mph. Furthermore, by 1934, in the US, Burlington's *Zephyr* had reached 112.5mph, but Gresley maintained his belief steam could do the job just as well.

Apparently, so did the Germans. On May 11, 1936, Deutsche Reichsbahn-Gesellschaft's streamlined 4-6-4 No. 05002 hit 124mph on the Berlin to Hamburg line – beating anything Gresley or Stanier had managed.

The problem with running faster and faster is braking distance become longer: first and foremost,

German Class 05 4-6-4 No. 05001, the surviving sister locomotive to No. 05003, which set a world steam railway speed record of 124mph in 1936 – and which Sir Nigel Gresley had set his sights on taking. What is not commonly known is on board that train were Heinrich Himmler and Reinhard Heydrich, two of the dregs of humanity who went on to use their country's railways to perpetuate the Holocaust. No. 05001 is now on permanent static displayed inside Nuremberg's Deutsche Bahn Museum. ROBIN JONES

braking systems had to be improved. Furthermore, signalling systems needed to be improved, and at the time, the East Coast Main Line did not have automatic signalling.

Gresley ran the rule over the Westinghouse system used by his rival the LMS, and arranged a series of trials, which involved rapid acceleration followed by the brake test.

Gresley chose A4 No. 4468 *Mallard*

for the test. Outshopped from Doncaster Works on March 3, 1938, it was the first of the class to be fitted with the Kylchap double chimney and blastpipe, as earlier tested on A3 No. 2751 *Humorist*. This arrangement allowed smoke to be distributed more easily. *Mallard* also had the new Westinghouse QSA (Quick Service Application) brake valves fitted.

Further improvements to the streamlined shape of the A4 were made

The pinnacle of the world steam age: *Mallard* reaching 126mph on Stoke Bank as photographed by one of Gresley's lineside team on July 3, 1938. No apologies whatsoever for the blurred nature of this picture captured with the camera equipment of the day, for it tells a story like no other. NRM

Mallard heading north through Potters Bar on Sunday, July 3, 1938, on the outward journey of its history-making trip. K LEITCH/COLOUR RAIL

in order to reduce as far as possible the dispersal of smoke from the chimney at the front of the locomotive.

Gresley's staff worked with the National Physical Laboratory at Teddington with a one-twelfth scale model of *Mallard*, and after much trial and error, hit upon a simple solution purely by chance. A minor indentation in the plasticine at the rear of the chimney on the model sent the smoke clear of the engine. Gresley, then 62, and in failing health, was delighted at the result of the model experiment – and was therefore determined to beat both Stanier and the Germans.

While Newsome organised the requested special brake test, Gresley hand-picked his footplate crew for a 'secret mission' he had in mind.

Doncaster driver Duddington, who had looked after *Mallard* ever since it left the works, was renowned for pushing locomotives hard, and was to be joined by firemen Thomas Bray, who had also been with No. 4468 from the outset. It was Gresley himself who chose *Mallard* for the test.

In late June, the pair were informed by Gresley's King's Cross office to prepare themselves for this special mission, but were not told what it was.

Newsome had arranged that three twin-car sets from the LNER 'Coronation' stock would take part, along with the luxurious 1906-built North Eastern Railway teak dynamometer car No. 902502, giving a total train weight of 240 tons.

During the preparation for the tests, Gresley revealed to his deputy Douglass Edge the real aim of the exercise and the reason behind the brake tests.

SECRECY TO THE LAST

On July 3, the Westinghouse breaking team arrived at Wood Green waterworks sidings in London to find a pristine *Mallard*, which had arrived at King's Cross the day before, coupled to the dynamometer car.

Sadly, Gresley was ill and unable attend, and was instead represented by Edge. Newsome was also on board, as was Bernard Atkinson from the locomotive running department, and Eric Bannister, who had helped find the solution to the smoke problem at the testing laboratory.

Yet, the real purpose of the mission was not revealed to the footplate crew, inspector Sam Jenkins, or the Westinghouse team, until the train had left Wood Green at 11.46am.

The outward journey involved a series of standard brake tests between 90-100mph, with Denis Carling, the LNER test inspector, overseeing the recording in the dynamometer car. The run ended as intended at Barkston, a few miles north of Grantham, where the branch to Sleaford and Boston left the main line. There, *Mallard* and the dynamometer car were turned on the triangle.

It had been worked out that a good run south from Barkston would give the A4 the chance to climb Stoke Bank at speed, with the record being attempted on the downward grade.

The train arrived at Barkston at 2.49pm prior to those on board having had lunch in the restaurant car. Sam Jenkins then tested a special intercom which had been set up between *Mallard's* cab and the dynamometer car.

Edge then summoned the Westinghouse team members and told them what was really going on – and it was far from carrying out run-of-the-mill braking tests.

He offered each of them a free taxi to Peterborough if they did not want to ride on the train as it attempted to retake the speed record on the way back south, down Stoke Bank, where nearly four years earlier *Flying Scotsman* had officially reached 100mph.

Every one of them refused. They knew they would be helping to make history, and nobody was prepared to back out of the chance of making it happen.

THE DEFINING PEAK MOMENT

The train departed from Barkston South Junction at 4.15pm, when tea was served in the First Class section.

The footplate crew were dismayed to find speed limits in force at Grantham because of permanent way work, with platelayers carrying out Sunday track maintenance, and the station was passed at just 18mph, instead of the usual 60-70mph for express trains. However, fireman Bray made full use of the time to build a big fire.

Gresley had earlier been told about a "dead slow speed restriction at Grantham", but nonetheless insisted the record attempt should still go ahead.

Bob Gwynne, assistant curator of rail vehicles at the National Railway Museum, commented: "Duddington climbed into the cab, turned his cap around (as had George Formby in the contemporary film No Limit), and drove *Mallard* into the history books.

"He had 27 years on the footplate, and had once driven the 'Scarborough Flyer' for 144 miles at over 74mph (average speed), considered at the time to be the highest speed ever maintained by steam in the UK."

Despite running at just 25mph at the beginning of the climb to Stoke Bank, the undaunted Duddington soon got *Mallard* up to 65mph, with its boiler at full pressure.

The engine accelerated up to Stoke summit and passed Stoke signalbox at 85mph.

The train then entered Stoke Tunnel, and before the guard switched on the lights, passengers were delighted by a firework display of red-hot cinders passing the windows after flying from *Mallard's* twin chimneys.

The record keepers inside the dynamometer car saw that the A4 had passed Stoke summit at 6mph faster than sister A4 No. 2512 *Silver Fox* when it had set its 113mph record at the same spot on August 27, 1936.

Mallard then accelerated down Stoke

Bank, faster than Silver Fox had done.

Within minutes, the speedometer reached 120mph, beating the LMS record.

Yet Duddington and Bray knew they had to do more inside the coming minutes, before the train would have to slow down at the Essendine curves.

For a quarter of a mile, the needle in the dynamometer car recorded 126mph, at milepost 90¼, between Little Bytham and Essendine, 90 miles and 220 yards from King's Cross. And for a split second, 126.1mph was recorded over just 60 yards.

The German record had now been broken as well, and would never be reclaimed.

It was recorded the train shook violently and crockery smashed to

the floor – and windows were broken in Little Bytham station as *Mallard* powered through, spraying the platform with hot ashes.

Edge was asked if the crew should try to go one better and hit 130mph, but with Essendine Tunnel approaching, he took the decision not to risk it.

Through the intercom, the message was conveyed to Duddington to shut off.

Essendine station was still passed at 108mph.

Minutes later, a distinctive smell indicated all was not well with *Mallard*. The A4's big middle big end bearing had run hot while developing 3000 cylinder hp, and needed to slow down as much as possible to reach Peterborough to avoid the locomotive being wrecked.

At Peterborough, it was discovered the white metal had melted. *Mallard* was taken off the train and Ivatt Atlantic No. 3290 returned it to King's Cross.

Light years away from the days when the GWR kept quiet about *City of Truro's* purported 102.3mph on Wellington Bank, the national press had been tipped off about the 126mph record, and were ready and waiting on the platform.

There, the footplate crew received a heroes' welcome. News of their feat made headlines, firstly throughout Britain and then around the world, within hours of the train arriving back in London. Journalists were taken into the dynamometer car, where they were shown the physical proof of the speed record.

Duddington and Jenkins were quoted as saying they thought a speed of 130mph would have been possible

Long-closed Little Bytham station, inside which it was claimed windows were shattered as *Mallard* roared through on its record run.

if the train had not had to slow for the junctions at Essendine

For days, the footplate crew were feted as celebrities, just like rock stars today, yet Duddington and Bray considered the record run to be all in a day's work and little more. The next day, the dynamic duo were back at work on the footplate of another East Coast Main Line express.

The press called *Mallard* the 'Blue Streak', the second word of which becoming a nickname applied ever since to the A4s.

Edge telephoned Gresley to convey

Heroes: The victorious *Mallard* crew (from left to right): driver Joe Duddington, fireman Tommy Bray, inspector Sam Jenkins, the train guard, and other members of the team at Peterborough after setting a new world record on July 3, 1938. NRM

As BR No. 60022, *Mallard* passes Darlington with the last steam-hauled northbound run of the 'Elizabethan' in September 1961. 4975DARWIN*

Mallard carrying its transitional number E22 at King's Cross in 1948. It was one of three Gresley A4 Pacifics chosen for the 1948 Exchange Trials, comparing the performance of the best engines of the 'Big Four' railways on each other's systems soon after Nationalisation. On the left is one of the N2 0-6-2Ts and on the right an N1 0-6-2T – the workhorses of suburban and empty stock duties. BEN BROOKSBANK*

the news. However, Gresley would not accept the 126mph as a reliable measurement and so 125mph was the figure published. Yet, *Mallard* had also maintained 120mph over three miles, a magnificent feat in itself.

So a new and immortal legend was born, and it was just what Britain needed after the doldrums of the Thirties in the wake of the Great Depression and the aftershock of the 1929 Wall Street Crash, which resulted in the rise of authoritarian regimes elsewhere with eventual catastrophic consequences.

Inside the cab of *Mallard*, as seen at the National Railway Museum in May 2013. ROBIN JONES

Gresley, *Mallard*, Duddington and Bray had shown the world it was indeed possible for Britain to achieve again, and come out on top of the world.

Mallard's run was also the peak of the great glamorous expresses which highlighted what many see as the zenith of the steam era.

Over in Hitler's Germany, both newspapers and Nazi party officials were at first silent about *Mallard's* feat, but eventually made the excuse it had taken the world steam record only because it had been running downhill, whereas their locomotive had done 124.5mph on the flat.

Yet, no firm and fast rules had ever been set for speed records. Mathematics could not hide the fact *Mallard* was, and still is, the fastest.

The overheated bearing was quickly re-metalled and *Mallard* returned to service nine days later.

There will forever be speculation as to what might have happened if the Sunday speed restriction had not been in place at Grantham. It was considered had that been the case, 130mph could have been achieved. It had been speculated that even before *Mallard's* run, such a speed would be possible with an A4.

Gresley wanted to try to set another new record the following year, but his ambition was scuppered by the build-up

The plaque fixed to *Mallard* in honour of its world steam speed record.

to and outbreak of the Second World War.

Ten years later, at the time of the 1948 Locomotive Exchanges, in which *Mallard* took part as No. E22, commemorative plaques were fixed to the sides of the loco, which stated that 126mph had been reached.

This figure has been the speed generally accepted ever since.

This sign stands at Stoke Bank to mark the spot where *Mallard* set a new world steam speed record. ROBIN JONES

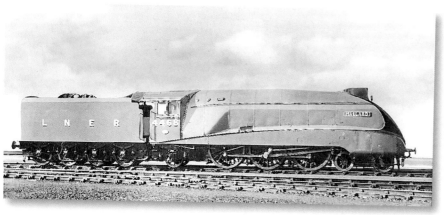

A postcard view of *Mallard* taken in the years following its record run. ROBIN JONES COLLECTION

Mallard on static display inside the National Railway Museum. ROBIN JONES

Mallard running through Seer Green, in the Chiltern Hills, with a special on November 2, 1986. JOHN TITLOW

The line-up of all six surviving A4 Pacifics inside the Great Hall at the National Railway Museum on October 26, 2013, for the Autumn Great Gathering, the second of three such reunions. From left, they are Nos. 60007, 60008, 6009, 4464, 4468 and 4469. The event attracted visitors from across the world, and was considered to be one of the most successful in the heritage railway sector. ROBIN JONES

SAVED BY ITS RECORD

In British Railways days regular steam-hauled rail services in the UK were officially limited to a 90mph line speed.

Mallard covered almost 1,500,000 miles before it was retired from service on April 23, 1963. Its duties had involved turns on the 'Elizabethan', a flagship express that ran non-stop over the 393 miles between King's Cross and Edinburgh Waverley from 1953 to the mid-1960s. Until September 8, 1961, 'Elizabethan' was steam-hauled, and in its day was the longest non-stop run in the world. The crews were able to change over mid-journey by using a corridor tender. Only a few locomotives other than *Mallard* had such a tender.

Because of its world record, *Mallard* was selected for preservation as part of the National Collection, over and above the first streamlined A4 class member –

Silver Link – which unfortunately was scrapped at Doncaster Works in 1963 after withdrawal.

Mallard was restored to working order in the 1980s, but has not operated since, apart from hauling some specials between York and Scarborough in July 1986 and two runs between York and Harrogate/Leeds around Easter 1987, and the 'Postal Pullman Marylebone to Banbury in 1988, to promote a special commemorative postage stamp. Since then, it has remained on static display

On July 3, 2013, *Mallard* celebrated 75 years since achieving the world speed record, and to help commemorate this date all six surviving A4 were brought together around the turntable in the Great Hall of the National Railway Museum at York for the first of three 'Great Gatherings', orchestrated by former museum head Steve Davies, who

The special stamp issued in 1988 to mark the 50th anniversary of the world record run. ROBIN JONES

admirably succeeded where others had failed.

He managed to persuade the two North American museums that owned No. 60008 *Dwight D. Eisenhower* and No. 60010 *Dominion of Canada* to loan them for the event, in return for cosmetic restoration in the NRM's workshops. They and *Mallard* were joined by the UK-based privately owned trio Nos. 4464 *Bittern*, 60007 *Sir Nigel Gresley* and 60009 *Union of South Africa*.

The question is being asked – will the museum steam *Mallard* again for the centenary of its world record run in 2038?

Known steam fan Prince Charles visited the National Railway Museum on July 22, 2013, for a private viewing of the Mallard 75 exhibition. He is seen looking out of the window of the A4, just as driver Joe Duddington would have done on the world speed record attempt on July 3, 1938. ROBIN JONES

A cake baked to mark the 75th anniversary of the world record run. ROBIN JONES

The dynamometer car positioned behind *Mallard* in the Great Hall of the National Railway Museum. ROBIN JONES

INSIDE THE CARRIAGE WHERE HISTORY WAS RECORDED

A rare glimpse inside a unique 'timewarp' vehicle that recorded world transport history was given by the National Railway Museum in December 2015.

Media representatives were given guided tours of NER dynamometer car No. 902502, the vehicle that recorded both *Flying Scotsman's* 100mph run on November 30, 1934, and *Mallard's* 126mph unbroken world record run on July 3, 1938.

The vehicle had undergone extensive remedial work by members of the museum's conservation team in readiness for the Stunts, Speed and Style exhibition, held the following spring.

The dynamometer car was built in 1905 at York Works, and ceased operation in December 1954. When positioned behind a moving locomotive, it enabled an on-board crew to measure and record a locomotive's speed and horsepower. The early 20th-century recording technology that is contained is effectively preserved in the same condition as when the records were set. The car is permanently displayed inside the museum's Great Hall, but the interior is not open to the public because of the delicate and priceless nature of the instruments it contains.

Bob Gwynne said: "The LNER dynamometer car is a crucial part of the *Flying Scotsman* story and of railway history more broadly. It tells the story of record-breaking steam stunts that are still renowned today."

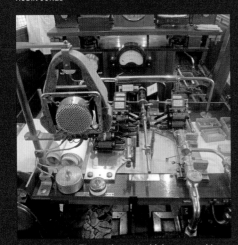

Those traveling inside the car in the 1930s on the record runs made by *Flying Scotsman* and *Mallard* watched history being made on these dials. ROBIN JONES

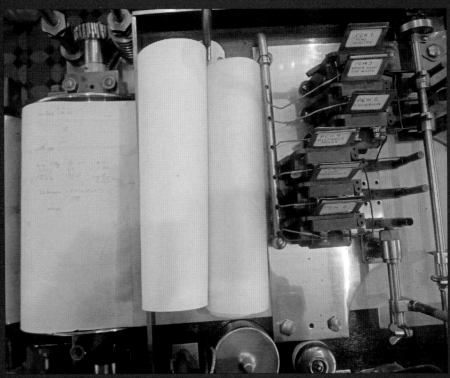

Frozen in time: The equipment which was used to record the historic locomotive runs. ROBIN JONES

The paper reels on which the speed records were transcribed by the recording equipment as they happened. ROBIN JONES

Chapter 11

Will the real *Thomas* please stand up?

The official Thomas the Tank Engine – Hudswell, Clarke 0-6-0T No. 1800 of 1947 – crosses the River Nene at Wansford on its Nene Valley Railway home.

As legendary locomotives go, vying for the No. 1 position must be that immortal children's favourite *Thomas the Tank Engine*. There are many restored steam locomotives today that bear its identity, but only one of them can claim to be the official 'Really Useful Engine'.

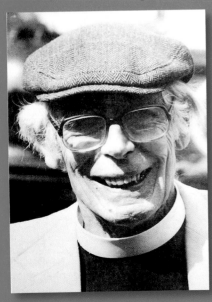

LEFT: The Rev Wilbert Awdry, creator of The Railway Series, pictured in 1982. He officially named Hudswell, Clarke 0-6-0T No. 1800 as *Thomas* in 1971. JAMIE SPILSBURY*

There can't be many railway enthusiasts who were not influenced by that little blue engine in any shape or form in their formative years.

Thomas the Tank Engine is instantly recognisable the world over. It may be no exaggeration to say that what Stephenson's *Rocket* is to transport, *Thomas No. 1* is to toys.

The creation of the Rev Wilbert Awdry, who inherited his deep interest in railways from his father, the Rev Vere Awdry, and together with his brother George became a keen railway modeller, made up a series of bedtime stories for his son Christopher, to amuse him during a bout of measles in 1943.

Encouraged by his wife, he began to commit them to paper, and his first book in what was to become The Railway Series was published in 1945.

By 1951, he had written four more, to the same formula: the adventures of railway locomotives based on real-life prototypes, all of which had human faces on their smokebox doors, and personalities to match, and which operated on the network covering the fictional Island of Sodor under the jurisdiction of Sir Topham Hatt, the Fat Controller. It is a statement of the blindingly obvious that history records the series proved phenomenally popular,

and not only spawned a series of books, toys, games and models, but a TV series and films into the bargain.

One of the most popular family events by far at heritage railways and museums in recent decades, not only in Britain but in countries around the world, are Thomas the Tank Engine or Days Out Thomas events. The concept has even expanded into theme parks, and is today a multi-million-pound earner on a scale the late Mr Awdry could never have envisaged.

Thomas the Tank Engine is indeed super legendary in terms of locomotives – but is he a creation of pure fiction?

While The Railway Series is colloquially referred to as 'the Thomas books' or the like, Thomas did not appear until Mr Awdry's second book, Thomas the Tank Engine. He was the subject of the four short stories inside, with his best friends *Percy* the saddle tank and *Toby* the tram engine. *Thomas* arrived on Sodor in 1915, when the Fat Controller bought him as a pilot engine. After rescuing *James* in Thomas & the Breakdown Train, he became a 'Really Useful Engine', and in the public eye went on to become the predominant character in the series.

In the real world, *Thomas* began life as a wooden toy created for Christopher Awdry (later lost in the USA). It carried the letters NW on its side tanks: Mr Awdry claimed this stood for "No Where".

Yet, as The Railway Series expanded, the network on which *Thomas* and his friends worked on became known as the North Western Railway.

The publisher of the second book in the series hired an illustrator for it –Reginald Payne. Mr Awdry chose a photograph of a real locomotive for him to work from when depicting *Thomas*, and picked one of a London, Brighton and South Coast Railway E2 class 0-6-0, a type designed by Lawson Billinton in 1913 for shunting and short-distance freight trains, the last one having been taken out of traffic by British Railways in 1963.

Around the same time that Mr Awdry was writing his second book in 1947, Hudswell, Clarke built 0-6-0T No. 1800. It spent its entire working life at the British Sugar Corporation's Peterborough plant pushing wagons of sugar beet up an incline until the day came when it was inevitably replaced by a diesel.

On March 28, 1969, the Peterborough branch of the East Anglian Locomotive Society was formed, with the aim of buying BR Standard Pacific No. 70000 *Britannia* and returning it to steam.

The previous year, another railway-minded vicar, the local Rev Richard Paten had bought BR Standard 5MT 4-6-0 No. 73050, initially to display it outside the city's technology college as a monument to tie in with Peterborough's railway history, but in 1971, it was moved to the British Sugar Corporation's (BSC) Fletton sidings for restoration.

Later that year, the society branch changed its name to Peterborough Railway Society, and developed the

Employed as a station pilot at London Victoria, LBSCR E2 0-6-0T No. 32104 is pictured at Stewarts Lane depot. The E2s were built in January 1914 and withdrawn in April 1963, and formed the basis of the original illustrations of *Thomas the Tank Engine*. BEN BROOKSBANK*

idea of setting up a heritage line on the doorstep, under the banner of the Nene Valley Railway.

In July that year, the society held an open day at the sugar factory, and No. 73050 appeared in steam for the first time in preservation. As an additional attraction, it was agreed the factory's tank engine could be painted in bright blue livery with red lining and carry a face on its smokebox. Not only that, but it was arranged for Mr Awdry to unveil the name *Thomas* on the side tank!

The Hudswell, Clarke loco continued to shunt the factory sidings during the following sugar beet season, still in blue livery, but without his face. When it finally retired, the BSC presented it to the society, and it has been a major attraction on the Nene Valley Railway – which proudly claims it to be the official physical manifestation of *Thomas the Tank Engine*, as it was named by its creator.

In 1979, British writer/producer Britt Allcroft arranged a deal to bring the stories to life as the TV series *Thomas the Tank Engine and Friends*, becoming an award-winning global hit, with a vast range of spin-off commercial products. The rights were subsequently acquired by HiT entertainment, which tried to sue the Nene Valley Railway on the grounds its *Thomas* locomotive was breaching their trademark.

The company lost the case as the court ruled it was not breaching HiT's trademark because No. 1800 was given the name *Thomas* by Mr Awdry.

After Mr Awdry retired in 1972, Christopher wrote more *Thomas* books, from his home in nearby Oundle.

Mr Awdry, who also became member No. 79 of the Talyllyn Railway Preservation Society, and based more fictional characters on that line's locomotive fleet, was awarded an OBE in the 1996 New Year's Honours List, but by that time his health had deteriorated and he was unable to travel to London. He died peacefully in Stroud, Gloucestershire, on March 21, 1997, aged 85.

No. 1800 again returned to steam in June 2016 following a two-and a-half-year overhaul, and is once again a major visitor draw on the Nene Valley Railway.

Meanwhile, other heritage railways have, with the permission of the rights' holder, repainted, remodelled and rebranded tank engines as *No.1 Thomas*, for use at their own money-spinning Thomas events, or for hire to other venues.

No. 1 Thomas the Tank Engine is seen approaching Caddaford curve on the South Devon Railway, working the 11.53am Caddaford-Buckfastleigh special on May 5, 2019. This hired-in 0-6-0T, a converted Hunslet Austerity saddle tank based on the Mid-Hants Railway, is one of many that masquerade as Thomas with permission of the rights' holder. COLIN WALLACE

Chapter 12

Stepney

"I believe from our file that your railway has an engine who adopts the persona of 'Stepney' at your Thomas events.

"If you would like this engine to be considered...can you pass a photograph and details on to me.

"If there is then a possibility of your engine being suitable for the event, the organisers will contact you direct with a view to hiring it...

"It is important for you to remember that this is a one-off occasion, and the engine cannot be hired out at any other time in its character guise, unless agreed..."

Those were the words of a promotions manager working for the company that in 2000 held the rights to the late Rev Wilbert Awdry's Thomas the Tank Engine series, in a letter addressed to Tim Baker, commercial director of the Bluebell Railway.

The letter was correct regarding the fact that the Sussex heritage line indeed has an 1875-built London, Brighton & South Coast Railway A1X 'Terrier' 0-6-0T in its fleet, and indeed, that locomotive does run as *Stepney* – not only during Thomas the Tank Engine events, but on every other day of the year.

And this locomotive never needs the slightest degree of contrivance to masquerade as a character from the Thomas series of books - because it is none other than the genuine *Stepney*!

Tim's reply to the rights holder's employee pointed out *Stepney* is the only locomotive in the Thomas series to have an identity synonymous with real life, and by no stretch of the imagination could be described as a fictional character, unlike the others in the books.

The 'Terriers' were designed by William Stroudley (March 6, 1833-December 20, 1889), one of the most famous steam locomotive engineers of the 19th century, who in 1870 was appointed locomotive superintendent of the LBSCR.

A total of 50 'Terriers' were built at Brighton Works between 1872-1880.

One of the most famous characters from children's railway books was never a fictional character, but a real-life locomotive that helped kick-start the preservation movement.

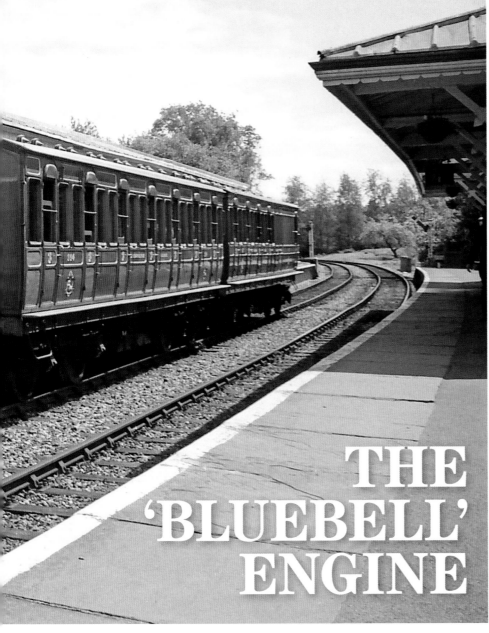

THE 'BLUEBELL' ENGINE

viaduct which it crossed over to reach the island, BR decided to withdraw the last remaining members of the class from traffic.

At the time of its withdrawal, following the closure of the line, No. 32636 (formerly No. 72 *Fenchurch*) was the oldest working steam engine in BR ownership.

Eight members of the class were bought privately for preservation, with two other examples being donated by BR to the Canadian Railway Museum and Britain's National Collection, now part of the National Railway Museum collection.

One of the eight, No. 55 *Stepney*, which had escaped an early round of withdrawals and scrapping by being

Originally nicknamed 'Rooters', they became widely known as 'Terriers' on account of the distinctive 'bark' of their exhaust beat.

Some 'Terriers' were sold to other operators after being displaced from their original workings out of London Bridge and London Victoria by more powerful locomotives, such as Stroudley's 'D1' 0-4-2Ts and the early stages of the LBSCR electrification schemes. Others were used on branch lines in Sussex and as shed pilots and shunters.

Class members passed into Southern Railway ownership following the Grouping of 1923, and while their numbers dwindled through scrapping,

many were inherited by British Railways in 1948, continuing to work into the early Sixties, most famously on the Hayling Island branch in Hampshire, which closed in November 1963.

With the closure of this line, not because it was losing money but because of the cost of upgrading the decaying

RIGHT: Madge Bessemer, the local spinster who delayed the closure of the Lewes to East Grinstead line, and inadvertently gave its would-be saviours time to save a section of the line as the Bluebell Railway, world famous as the home of *Stepney*, its first locomotive.

delegated to the Hayling Island branch, acquired fame as the first locomotive to arrive at the Bluebell Railway, which in August 1960 became the first heritage railway to open on a section of the closed BR network, and also for appearing in Stepney the Bluebell Engine, one of the books in the original Railway Series written by Mr Awdry.

THE PIONEERS WHO PAVED THE WAY

In 1951, the Talyllyn Railway became the first line in the world to be taken over by volunteer preservationists, and was closely followed by the reopening of the moribund Ffestiniog Railway, on a similar basis.

The Talyllyn milestone inspired The Titfield Thunderbolt, a 1953 Ealing comedy film, starring Stanley Holloway, George Relph and John Gregson, about a group of villagers trying to keep their branch line operating after British Railways decided to close it.

It helped sow the seeds of the idea it was possible to save a railway line from being closed, and you did not have to accept everything the powers that be dictated.

However, saving a seven-mile narrow gauge line was one matter: reviving a standard-gauge line with far bigger locomotives and stock was another.

The Bluebell Railway has its origins in the 1877 Act of Parliament, which authorised construction of the Lewes & East Grinstead Railway, acquired by the LBSCR a year later.

Both included the clause "four passenger trains each way daily to run on this line, with through connections at East Grinstead to London and to stop at Sheffield Bridges, Newick and West Hoathly". The clause imposed a legal requirement to provide a service and the only way to remove this obligation was to pass another Act.

In 1954, BR's branch line committee proposed closing the line from East Grinstead to Culver Junction, near Lewes. Despite a challenge by local residents, the closure was set for June 15, 1955, although it took place earlier, on May 29, because of a rail strike.

Local residents and rail users fought hard over the next three years to get the decision reversed.

Shortly after closure, Chailey spinster Madge Bessemer, the granddaughter of Henry Bessemer, inventor of the Bessemer converter for transforming pig iron into steel, discovered the clause in the 1877 and 1878 Acts relating to the 'Statutory Line' and demanded BR reinstate services.

Aided by local MP Tufton Beamish, she forced BR to think again. Faced with this statutory legal obligation, BR reopened the line on August 7, 1956, but with trains stopping only at stations mentioned in the Acts. Because of this, it became nicknamed the 'sulky service'.

BR took the case to the House of Commons in 1957, resulting in a public inquiry. BR was censured, but later the Transport Commission was able to persuade Parliament to repeal the special section of the Act, and so the line was finally closed on March 17, 1958.

On that final day, Madge Bessemer encountered Carshalton Technical College student Chris Campbell, who shared his many recollections of travelling on the line while spending school holidays with relatives. Inspired by her efforts to save the line, Chris, then 18, wondered if it might be possible he could take up the baton.

Meanwhile, Martin Eastland, 19, a telecommunications engineering student of nearby Haywards Heath; David Dallimore, a student at the London School of Economics, from Woodingdean'; and Brighton-based

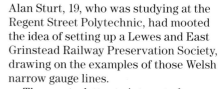

LBSCR A1X 'Terrier' 0-6-0T No. 55 *Stepney* leaves the crowded platforms at Sheffield Park with the first public Bluebell Railway passenger train on August 7, 1960. The Hayling Island branch veteran was the fledgling line's first locomotive.
BLUEBELL RAILWAY ARCHIVES

Alan Sturt, 19, who was studying at the Regent Street Polytechnic, had mooted the idea of setting up a Lewes and East Grinstead Railway Preservation Society, drawing on the examples of those Welsh narrow gauge lines.

They sent a letter to interested parties highlighting Madge Bessemer's campaign and the unexpected public support it had generated.

They initially hoped to save the entire route, reopening it stages at a time, acquiring a GWR railcar for regular use, and using steam during the summer months.

On March 15, 1959, a group that included future president of the society Bernard Holden MBE met in Ardingly and duly formed the Lewes and East Grinstead Railway Preservation Society. However, at the meeting, the society changed its name to the Bluebell Railway Preservation Society.

LBSCR 'Terrier' 0-6-0T No. 55 *Stepney* stands at the Bluebell Railway's Sheffield Park headquarters in the Stroudley golden ochre livery which made it world famous, largely because of its appearance in the Thomas the Tank Engine books. JON BOWERS/ BLUEBELL RAILWAY

It has been speculated that while picking spring flowers on the embankment near her estate, Madge Bessemer may have coined the nickname of the 'Bluebell Line'.

The society's initial and over-ambitious aim was to reopen the whole line from East Grinstead to Culver Junction as a commercial service. However, the society failed to buy the whole line, and had to severely cut its lofty ambitions down to size.

The society then came up with the idea of using the line between Sheffield Park and Horsted Keynes as a tourist attraction, with vintage locomotives and stock operated by unpaid volunteer staff.

From small and very ambitious beginnings, the idea blossomed into a major tourist attraction and a major centre for railway heritage, renowned the world over

RAILWAY SERIES, No. 18

STEPNEY
THE "BLUEBELL" ENGINE

THE REV. W. AWDRY

Stepney is the star of No. 18 in the Rev Wilbert Awdry's Railway Series, *Stepney* the 'Bluebell' Engine.

Founding members of the Bluebell Railway Preservation Society, formerly the Lewes & East Grinstead RPS, line up with the heritage line's first locomotive, No. 55 *Stepney*, at Kingscote on May 17, 2000. ROBIN JONES

THE BLUEBELL BUYS ITS FIRST ENGINE

As BR still ran the third-rail electrified line from Horsted Keynes to Ardingly, and could not run into Horsted Keynes itself, the society leased a stretch of track from just south of Horsted Keynes, and built the temporary Bluebell Halt, 100 yards to the south.

After being bought by the society straight out of service from BR on May 17, 1960, *Stepney* (as No. 32655) became the first engine to arrive at the Bluebell Railway, effectively making it the doyen of the standard-gauge heritage railway movement.

Following its purchase, the loco ran under its own steam from Brighton shed to Horsted Keynes, hauling the two carriages the revivalists also bought.

The trio had been bought from BR for £750 (£550 for the locomotive and £100 each for the carriages, which came from the Chesham branch), *Stepney* having just been overhauled at Eastleigh Works.

At Horsted Keynes, Bluebell officials signed the required indemnity, and the three were allowed to proceed to Sheffield Park.

On August 7, 1960, the first Bluebell Railway services ran from Bluebell Halt,

On May 17, 2000, the late Bluebell society president Bernard Holden MBE, 93, addressed guests and founding members at a VIP reception to mark the 40th anniversary of the arrival of *Stepney* and the first rolling stock on the line. The reception was held inside the Bessemer Arms, Sheffield Park station's modern restaurant, named after Madge Bessemer, the local spinster who fought BR to reopen the line after it originally closed, because of a legal technicality. Bernard chaired the first meeting to save the line in 1959 because the would-be revivalists were considered minors in law. He recalled how fast the purchase of *Stepney* took place. The deal was signed on May 2, 1960, with the locomotive arriving a fortnight later.

Some of the myriad of pocket-money-priced toys that have been produced over the decades on the back of *Stepney's* stardom in the Thomas the Tank Engine books.

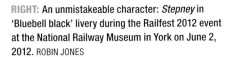

RIGHT: An unmistakeable character: *Stepney* in 'Bluebell black' livery during the Railfest 2012 event at the National Railway Museum in York on June 2, 2012. ROBIN JONES

100 yards south of Horsted Keynes, to Sheffield Park.

In 1962, the society extended its services into Horsted Keynes, and invited none other than East Grinstead resident Dr Richard Beeching – the BR chairman later immortalised as the 'axeman' who infamously recommended the closure of so much of the UK's rural rail network – to open a halt at Holywell (Waterworks).

Stepney was to return to action on the national network despite now being in private ownership, working two special trains over the Southern Region.

On October 21, 1962, *Stepney* double-headed with London & South Western Railway Adams radial tank No. 488 on the Haywards Heath to Horsted Keynes

RIGHT: A Brighton *Evening Argus* report the day after the arrival of *Stepney* and the two coaches at the Bluebell Railway on May 17, 1960.

branch and on the return leg of a railtour from London Victoria to the Bluebell Railway.

Furthermore, a special ran from Brighton to Horsted Keynes on October 27, 1963 for society members, with *Stepney* double-heading with LBSCR 0-6-2T No. 473 *Birch Grove*.

The train was run to mark the closure of the line from Haywards Heath to Horsted Keynes.

Holywell Halt closed within 12 months, and after BR withdrew its passenger services from Horsted Keynes to Haywards Heath, Bluebell trains could at last run into Horsted Keynes station.

With complete closure of the line of the line north of Horsted Keynes, the Bluebell Railway found itself severed from the BR system.

Had the Bluebell Railway not started its operations in 1960, the blueprint of what was possible in keeping the treasures of the steam era alive for future generations would not have been there for others to follow.

If the UK railway preservation movement had taken several more years to reach that stage, how many now-priceless examples of classic locomotives and rolling stock would have been lost forever?

Indeed, it was to be another eight years before the next former BR line to be reopened as a heritage line, the Keighley & Worth Valley Railway, ran its first public trains.

MORE FAME AND FURTHER FORTUNE

As well as appearing in Mr Awdry's books, *Stepney* also featured in the TV series of Thomas the Tank Engine & Friends. In it, he was rescued by Rusty the Diesel and also ran his own branch line running beside the Skarloey Railway.

A 1961 film version of Anna Karenina, parts of which were filmed on the Bluebell Railway, featured *Stepney*, disguised as a Russian locomotive.

Stepney appeared in the 1983 music video for singer Tracey Ullman's Move Over Darling.

On January 14, 2012, *Stepney* made an 'only-morning' appearance in BR lined black livery with the 'cycling lion' crest and as No. 32655, for a special photographic charter. It carried the same BR livery again on April 17, 2012 for another photographic charter, this time with the later 'ferret and dartboard' crest. It returned to Bluebell livery in time for its appearance in Railfest 2012 at the National Railway Museum in York in June 2012.

The following year, *Stepney* was to help make further Bluebell history. On an icy and snowbound March 23, 2013, it took part in the first public train over the Bluebell Railway's long-awaited seven-mile extension to East Grinstead, which allowed it to link up to the national network once more.

The push to the north had begun in 1974 when the society bought the site of

On March 23, 2017, the 'Sunny South' was anything but. LBSCR A1X 0-6-0T No. 55 *Stepney*, SECR P class 0-6-0T No. 323 *Bluebell* and LBSCR E4 0-6-2T No. 473 *Birch Grove* arrive at East Grinstead with the late-running empty stock to form the first departure from East Grinstead on the day of the public opening of the Bluebell Railway's northern extension, which was to prove a phenomenal success both for the heritage line and the town's tourist economy.
ANDREW STRONGITHARM

Class A1X Terrier No. 32678 and a 'birdcage' brake coach at Tenterden Town on the Kent & East Sussex Railway on June 11, 2011. PETER SKUCE*

SISTERS OF *STEPNEY*

A fifth of the 50-strong class of Stroudley 'Terriers' have been preserved.

Apart from *Stepney*, they are: No. 40 *Brighton* – now No. W11 at the Isle of Wight Steam Railway; No. 46 *Newington* – No. W8 *Freshwater* at the preserved Isle of Wight Steam Railway; No. 50 *Whitechapel* – No. 32650 *Sutton*, at the Spa Valley Railway; No. 54 *Waddon* – part of the Canadian Railway Museum collection; No. 62 *Martello* - at Bressingham Steam Museum, having been repainted as No. 662 *Martello* and later No. 32662; No. 70 *Poplar* – based on the Kent & East Sussex Railway, having taken the guise of No. 3 *Bodiam* and later No. 32670; No. 72 *Fenchurch* – No. 672 *Fenchurch*, and also at the Bluebell Railway; No. 78 *Knowle* – No. 32678, at the Kent & East Sussex Railway; and No. 82 *Boxhill*, at the National Railway Museum.

the demolished West Hoathly station, and Kingscote station was bought in January 1985. Despite opposition from local councillors, a public inquiry resulted in both the Secretaries of State for the Environment and Transport giving planning permission and a Light Railway Order for an extension to East Grinstead that year.

Work on the seven-mile extension from Horsted Keynes to East Grinstead began on March 13, 1988 with a golden spike ceremony. The extension from Horsted Keynes as far as Kingscote was completed in 1994, including the relaying of track through the 731-yard Sharpthorne Tunnel. However, the biggest obstacle was the 30ft-deep, 1600ft-long Imberhorne cutting, which after the original line was lifted had been used as a landfill site for domestic waste. At a cost of £5 million, around 96,000 cubic metres of non-toxic waste was taken out by rail to a landfill site to the north of Aylesbury.

The first public train from East Grinstead was hauled by a trio headed by E4 No. 473, aka *Birch Grove*, in Southern green livery, followed by blue-liveried SECR P 0-6-0T No. 323 *Bluebell* and No. 55 *Stepney*, which hauled that first train back in 1960.

Stepney's main steam pipe failed

Stepney at Freshfield Bank on November 4, 2006.
JON BOWERS/BLUEBELL RAILWAY

in early 2014, and was subsequently repainted into its traditional Stroudley golden ochre livery for static display. It can now be seen in the SteamWorks! exhibition at Sheffield Park station.

At its next major overhaul, *Stepney* will need new cylinders, the castings for which are already made, substantial work on the frames and major boiler repairs. The Stepney Club is run for the benefit of the railway's youngest admirers aged three to eight years old.

Decades of fame has seen *Stepney* reproduced as numerous models and toys for all ages, and the Bluebell Railway does not have to pay the Thomas the Tank Engine rights holder royalties – No. 55 appears as itself!

Chapter 13

LIVING THE LEGEND:

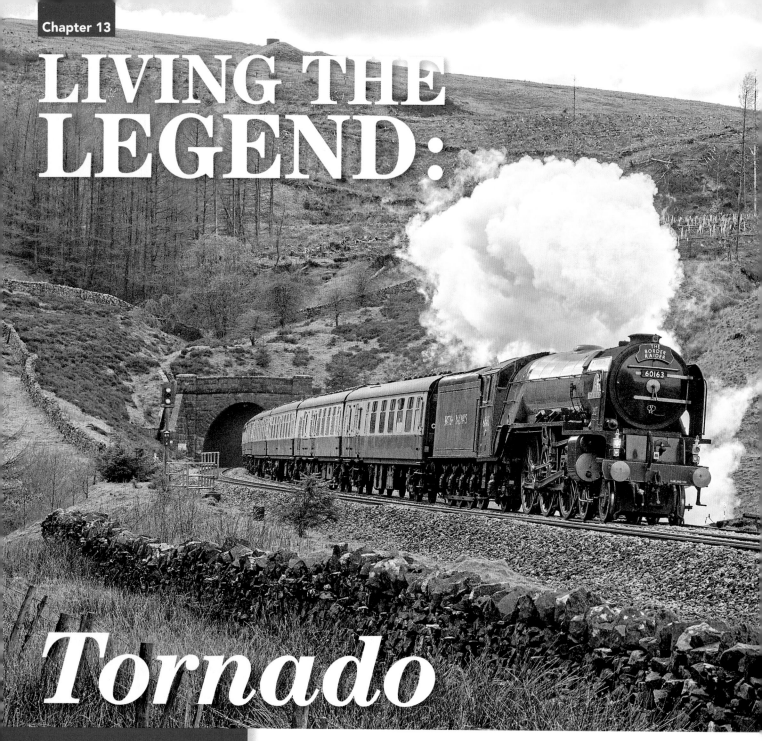

Tornado

We have seen classic locomotives from the history books that have long-since acquired legendary status, but one that was officially launched as recently as 2009 is boosting Britain's proud steam heritage by the year

TOP: A1 Peppercorn Pacific No. 60163 *Tornado* heads UK Railtours 'Border Raider' trip through Dent Head on the Settle and Carlisle line on April 13. MICHAEL ANDERSON

THIS volume contains just a few of the many stories about locomotives which became defining legends of the steam era and inspired countless generations, whether it be the results of the vision of the early inventors, the derring-do of footplate crews in breaking steam records or the chief mechanical engineers who took design to new limits with the backing of major railway works.

We have all been enthralled by those tales of national newspapermen waiting at London termini to greet drivers and firemen on the likes of *Princess Elizabeth*, *Flying Scotsman* and *Mallard*, stories we believed have been long since consigned to the history books, and which we can never experience again for ourselves.

However, they are happening again – right here in the 21st century.

Imagine a group of friends who reminisce about a legendary locomotive that has long since disappeared into the pages of history, and who draw up a hair-brained scheme on the back of a beermat to not only bring it back to life again but have it running express charters trains all over the national network, and reaching a speed in excess of 100mph. A story stranger than fiction - surely one only the likes of Jules Verne could concoct?

Yet it happened – and provided us with a locomotive of the magnitude of *Flying Scotsman* in the 21st century.

The 50th Peppercorn A1 Pacific No. 60163 *Tornado*, took nearly two decades to build, at a cost of £3million, and has become a flagship of the heritage railway sector. Just like *Flying Scotsman*, it has continued to draw crowds wherever it goes, and is a perfect example of the principle that railway

0-6-0ST No. 3890 of 1964, which now runs at the Buckinghamshire Railway Centre.

The first new steam locomotive built for the heritage sector was the 15in-gauge Ravenglass & Eskdale Railway's 2-8-2 *River Mite*, constructed by Clarkson of York in 1966 to the design of a Gresley P1, but there are those who would hold it still falls within the 'miniature' category. As stated earlier, the first 'full-size' new build was the Ffestiniog Railway's double Fairlie *Earl of Merioneth*, built at the line's Boston Lodge Works in 1979.

HOW MONEY TALKED AND DELIVERED

Raw enthusiasm was never going to build a full-size 4-6-2, and never will. The phenomenal success of The A1 Steam Locomotive Trust was in harnessing that raw enthusiasm from as wide a field as possible and turning it into hard currency and bank vaults full of it. No amount of raffle tickets, souvenir calendars and pens or car boot sales would raise even a fraction of the colossal amount of money needed for such a project.

North East businessman David Champion, the project's driving force through much of the 1990s, worked out if 1000 people could be persuaded to donate £1.25 a week (or £5 a month), it would take 'only' 10 years to raise that amount of money, allowing for charity Gift Aid, and so – under the now-famous phrase: "An A1 for the price of a pint!" – the concept of the regular donor or covenantor was born. Thanks entirely to this approach from the outset, today we can marvel at and ride behind a Peppercorn A1 again.

HOW THE JIGSAW CAME TOGETHER

A large collection of LNER drawings from Doncaster Works held in the National Railway Museum formed the basis of the plans for the new A1, drawn up under the auspices of the trust's project engineer David Elliott, who unlike Arthur H Peppercorn had the distinct advance of digital scanning technology.

In 1994 none other than the late widow of Peppercorn, Dorothy Mather, pressed the button on the state-of-the-art plasma cutting machine at BSD's Leeds plant to cut the main frames of the locomotive, which according to railway tradition, from that moment officially existed. Dorothy became honorary president of the trust, forming a unique link between the steam eras of the past and the future.

Sheffield-based steel manufacturer William Cook Cast Products, produced the main driving wheels for the loco on extremely generous terms.

The name *Tornado* was chosen in

Dorothy Mather, the widow of A1 designed Arthur H Peppercorn, lights the first fire in *Tornado's* grate at Darlington Locomotive Works on January 9, 2008. ROBIN JONES

honour of the RAF Tornado air crews in the Gulf War. In January 1995, RAF officers presented a pair of nameplates to the trust during the frame-laying ceremony at Tyseley Locomotive Works, where the first stages of assembly of No. 60163 took place before the trust turned the historic former Hopetown carriage works of the Stockton & Darlington Railway in Darlington into its permanent HQ from 1997 onwards.

The trust launched a bearer bond scheme to raise the £500,000 boiler to be built by Germany's Meiningen locomotive works, and it was lifted onto *Tornado's* rolling chassis at Darlington in June 2007.

January 9, 2008 saw Dorothy Mather light the first fire in Tornado's grate and the trust made much of the attendance publicity. BBC TV news were first to pick up the story, and gave the new legend wheels.

On Friday, August 1, 2008 a crowd of international journalists descended on the works to watch *Tornado* run along a short stretch of track, with Dorothy proudly standing on the footplate.

Still in plain works grey primer with the A1 Trust's website address www.a1steam.com emblazoned on the tender sides, *Tornado* then undertook two months of running in and official inspections on the Great Central Railway at Loughborough, and even appeared with a face during a Thomas the Tank Engine event.

Its first passenger train was run on Sunday, September, 21, when around 1000 covenantors and their guests were allocated seats in an exclusive train undertaking several round trips of the heritage line, as crowds gathered at every vantage point; they would be the first of many.

Tornado was then taken to the

preservation so often proves itself to be the art of the possible.

From small acorns grow mighty oaks. On March 24, 1990, a group of enthusiasts in the North East held an informal discussion about plugging one of the biggest gaps in the British heritage steam locomotive fleet, that of a Peppercorn A1. A public meeting was held on April 28 that year, chaired by the group's first chairman Mike Wilson, and The A1 Steam locomotive Trust was formally launched on November 17, to attempt a project that many observers remained steadfast in their opinion "couldn't be done".

The previous steam locomotive built for the main line was BR Standard 9F 2-10-0 No. 92220 *Evening Star*, which emerged from Swindon in 1960. The final standard-gauge steam locomotive built for UK use in the steam era, albeit industrial only, was Hunslet Austerity

Tornado, still in grey works primer, heads its first passenger train on the Great Central Railway on September 21, 2008. ROBIN JONES

Tornado hauling the Royal Train through Church Fenton, North Yorkshire, following its naming on February 19, 2009 by the Prince of Wales, whose motif is displayed on the smokebox. GEOFF GRIFFITHS/A1SLT

National Railway Museum from where it ran a series of main line test runs, the first to Scarborough on the evening of November 4, 2008, without any advance publicity. However, backed by the internet, the enthusiast rumour mill went into overdrive and hundreds turned out to gaze in awe.

For these runs, *Tornado* had a maximum permitted speed of 75mph, but history repeated itself. As with *City of Truro's* purported 102.3mph in 1904, when the railway authorities kept quiet about it for many years afterwards, it was not until October 2013 driver Dave Court publicly admitted he took No. 60163 to 90mph twice on its third test run, between Newcastle and York on November 18, 2008, without dispensation being obtained. He was suspended for speeding as a result.

Early December 2008, in the National Railway Museum's workshop, *Tornado* was painted in BR apple green and lined out, with BRITISH RAILWAYS in capital letters on the tender, a livery carried by the first 30 of the 49 original A1s back in 1948.

THE NEW STEEL CELEBRITY – WITH ROYAL APPROVAL

Saturday, January 31, 2009 saw the 'mission impossible' finally prove itself to be possible when *Tornado* hauled its first public main line passenger run, the 'Peppercorn Pioneer', an exclusive inaugural trip for covenantors, from York to Newcastle-on-Tyne and back, evoking memories of the final journey made by the last original A1, failed preservation target No. 60145 *St Mungo*, on December 31, 1965.

Every vantage point on the East Coast Main Line between the two cities was packed with parked cars, photographers and ordinary members of the public eager to glimpse this new national media celebrity.

At York, the *Tornado* sounded its whistle as it prepared to begin its journey at 12.07pm, hauling 13 carriages weighing a total of 550 tons behind it.

As it pulled out of York, a huge cheer rose from the delighted masses, and on its return to the footplate crew were, like the predecessors in similar landmark feats in the 'real' steam era, afforded a heroes' welcome by all. *Flying Scotsman* was a few hundred yards away, in pieces in the museum's workshops, while the 'young pretender' was stealing its crown!

On Saturday, February 7, 2009 the ordinary fare-paying public rode for the first time behind *Tornado*, which made a triumphant first entry into King's Cross, heading 'The Talisman' from Darlington.

On February 19, 2009, *Tornado* was officially named and launched into traffic by the Princes of Wales and the Duchess of Cornwall on platform 9 at York station before it performed the rare honour of hauling the Royal Train to Leeds, as again, thousands of onlookers packed the platforms. Dorothy was introduced to the royal couple, while Prince Charles was presented with an OO scale model of *Tornado* in a glass case, before donning a boiler jacket and boarding the cab, where the crew showed him the controls.

On February 28, *Tornado* made its first journey into Scotland with 'The Auld Reekie Express' from York

to Edinburgh, and on March 7, became the first A1 to depart from Edinburgh for 40 years with the 'North Briton' from Edinburgh to York.

LANDMARKS FURIOUS AND FAST

Tornado became a staple feature of the main line scene, with regular trips, eager crowds of onlookers and packed station platforms over overbridges becoming the norm.

Saturday, April 25, 2009 saw *Tornado* become the star of BBC's Top Gear three-way race between a Jaguar XK120 car, a Vincent Black Shadow motorbike and the A1, all designs of 1949, from London to Edinburgh.

Tornado, with the programme's then presenter Jeremy Clarkson on the footplate, arrived one minute ahead of schedule at Waverley at 3.26 pm, having taken a total of eight hours exactly. He ran the short distance to the Balmoral Hotel, only to find his colleague James May, who had driven the Jaguar, was already there, having arrived 10 minutes earlier. Fellow presenter Richard Hammond's motorbike had broken down en route. The escapade was broadcast on June 21, 2009, expanding *Tornado's* audience to tens of millions more people worldwide.

On May 23 that year, the Institution of Mechanical Engineers presented *Tornado* with an Engineering Heritage Award at York, and on July 5, No. 60163

Heading the 'Scarborough Flyer', *Tornado* arrives at the resort on June 4, 2016. ROBIN JONES

Prince Charles in the cab of *Tornado* after officially naming it at York station on February 19, 2009. ROBIN JONES

clocked up 10,000 miles while hauling the 'Torbay Express'.

On Friday, September 4, 2009, *Tornado* hauled the British leg of a three-day re-creation of a mercy trip from Prague made 70 years earlier, when British stock exchange clerk the late Sir Nicholas Winton arranged a 'Kindertransport' train to take hundreds of Jewish children from Nazi-occupied Europe to safety. At Liverpool Street station, Sir Nicholas, then 100 years old, boarded the A1's footplate after being reunited with more than 20 of the children he saved from the Holocaust.

REAL STEAM TO THE RESCUE

On December 21, 2009, *Tornado* rescued stranded commuters with its 'The White Cliffs' Christmas tour after Kent's railways shut down following heavy snowfall, with regular EMUs unable to cope and the Eurostar trains frozen inside the Channel Tunnel.

Thursday, June 24, 2010 saw *Tornado* set a new record, this time on the West Coast Main Line. By 19 seconds, it beat the previous record set in 1995 by

Late September 2016 saw *Tornado* united with none other than *Flying Scotsman* for the Severn Valley Railway's special Pacific Power gala. No. 60163 is seen departing from Highley station for Bewdley on September 21. ROBIN JONES

unique BR 8P Pacific No. 71000 *Duke of Gloucester* for running over Shap summit, with the A1 Trust's 13-coach 'Border Raider'. *Tornado* breasted the legendary summit at 43.5mph, averaging 61.3mph from the non-stop leg from Preston to Carlisle.

On September 13, 2015, *Tornado*

made its first trip, over the new Borders Railway –the £294m 30½-mile rebuilt northernmost third of the 98-mile Waverley Route, four days after it had been officially opened by HM Queen – when it hauled a ScotRail special from Edinburgh Waverley to Tweedbank, the line's new terminus.

TON-UP *TORNADO*

At 3.42am on Wednesday, April 12, 2017, railway heritage-era history was made, when *Tornado* reached 101mph during a 90mph proving run.

With a select group of invited guests on board the nine-coach train, the locomotive was undertaking tests between Doncaster and Newcastle in view of raising its permitted maximum speed to give more flexibility to future charter planning.

Limited to 75mph, The A1 Steam Locomotive Trust sought to increase the maximum speed to 90mph to bring it in line with other trains on the network.

Tornado back at Doncaster after the early-hours run which saw it reach 101mph while returning from Newcastle-upon-Tyne.

The mobile telephone app which recorded *Tornado's* speed on Wednesday, April 12, 2017 as 101mph correlated to recording data from equipment in the locomotive's cab. ROBIN JONES

The tests were organised in partnership with DB Cargo Rail and Network Rail, and took place with rail industry engineers and certification bodies monitoring the trial.

During testing the locomotive was fitted with diagnostic measurement equipment and, as is customary for safety reasons, it had to operate at 10% above its planned maximum speed.

On the return leg from Newcastle Central to Doncaster, instruments measured a speed of between 100.5mph and 101mph between Raskelf and Alne on the approach to York.

The ground-breaking test saw the first 100mph run by a steam locomotive in the UK for half a century, beating LNER A4 Pacific No. 4464 *Bittern's* claimed 94.5mph, set in December 2013.

The cover-of-darkness test run was carried out with a blanket ban on prior publicity for fear of drawing lineside trespassers, so unlike the halcyon days of steam there were no waiting pressman with oversize flashbulbs on the platform at the journey's end.

In 2017, I was able to jump off the train straight into my car back at Doncaster station. It started with the simple turn of the key, and minutes later I was at the first available wi-fi hotspot, and broadcasting the latest British triumph to an unsuspecting world before dawn via *Heritage Railway* magazine's facebook. com/heritagerailway page, with nearly a third of a million followers across the globe.

Nigel Gresley and Arthur H Peppercorn may well have approved!

Will this become one of the most iconic images of the railway heritage sector? Three of the retiring RAF Tornado jets swoop over the 21st century locomotive that was named in their honour as it stands near Leeming Bar on the Wensleydale Railway. The picture appeared in national newspapers and many other media outlets the following day, giving yet more publicity to the locomotive.
MANDY GRANT/A1SLT

A WHIRLWIND THROUGH THE DALE

Sadly, while heading its first public 90mph tour, the trust's 'Ebor Flyer' from King's Cross to York on April 14, 2018, *Tornado* failed after hitting 91mph north of Arlesley. The train ground to a halt at Sandy, 43 miles out of London, and the stricken A1 was towed to the Nene Valley Railway at Peterborough, where it spent many months undergoing tests and repairs on the line's Wansford shed. An examination indicated the problem was caused by a lack of lubrication rather than speed.

However, it was considered sufficiently fit to appear on the Wensleydale Railway during February 15-17, 2019, honouring a previous commitment. The visit again underlined the proven crowd-pulling appeal of the celebrity locomotive

A total of 1039 passengers were carried on four *Tornado* trains. Each of the trains was full, with 260 passengers each. Two extra carriages were added on the Sunday to meet demand, so eight were hauled in total.

A Valentine's afternoon tea service on the 17th was sold out. It carried 122 passengers, and an extra coach was added.

A special *Tornado* beer was brought in from Scotland, and all 100 bottles were sold.

Such commercial dividends would do even the larger heritage lines proud.

As stated earlier, the name *Tornado* was chosen in honour of the RAF air crews flying at the time in the Gulf War, in which the jet aircraft were first used

Tornado in action on the Wensleydale Railway during its hugely successful February 2019 visit.
MANDY GRANT/A1SLT

in combat. The honour of choosing the name was given to a £50,000 sponsor of the project.

Accordingly, at Wensleydale on the afternoon of Tuesday, February 19, *Tornado* the locomotive gave a steamy farewell to its airborne namesake, as they flew over the A1, near Leeming Bar.

The aircraft were on the first of a three-day series of 'finale flypasts' during a final tour of the UK that flew

over most RAF bases and other key sites associated with the aircraft.

The jets were taken out of service at the end of March 2019.

However, *Tornado* proved it was a long way from retirement. In the wake of its first Wensleydale visit, the loco passed its main line proving run.

It will undoubtedly delight crowds for many more years, even decades, to come.

2007 PRINCE OF WALES
Building Britain's Most Powerful Steam Locomotive

Follow us on

WILLIAM COOK
CAST PRODUCTS
Principal Sponsor of The A1 Steam Locomotive Trust

Building Britain's most powerful steam locomotive - it's time to get on-board

In only five years the P2 Project has over £2m spent, £2.5m raised and £3.2m pledged, almost 1,000 regular donors (Covenantors), engine wheelsets fitted & frames erected, over 150 steel casting delivered, the smokebox & cab fitted, the boiler cladding completed and the electrical system order placed – but there is still a long way to go. With your support the next 12 months will see the delivery of the heavy motion and the completion of the tender frames & tank. The cylinder block and boiler will be ordered.

We still need to raise £5m to complete new Gresley class P2 No. 2007 *Prince of Wales*. YOU can help to make this a reality sooner rather than later. A P2 for the price of a pint of beer a week - become a regular Covenantor from only £10.00 per month.

To find out more visit www.p2steam.com, email enquiries@p2steam.com or call 01325 460163 today.

P2 Construction Fund, The A1 Steam Locomotive Trust, Darlington Locomotive Works, Hopetown Lane, Darlington, DL3 6RQ

From the builders, owners and operators of new 100mph main line steam locomotive No. 60163 Tornado

Chapter 14

Clun Castle:

FLAGSHIP OF A NEW STEAM EMPIRE

Not only did WR 4-6-0 No. 7029 *Clun Castle* bathe in glory on a 60th anniversary special to mark *City of Truro's* unofficial world record feat, it hauled the last British Rail steam train out of Paddington. And then, sold into preservation, it laid the foundation for what is now Tyseley Locomotive Works and Vintage Trains, which in 2019 became Britain's newest Train Operating Company.

Western Region 4-6-0 No. 7029 *Clun Castle* was given a hero's welcome as it made its first public movements for many years at an exclusive VIP launch following overhaul.

Shortly after 11am on Saturday, October 28, 2017, the 1950-built Swindon product, outshopped in gleaming Brunswick green, received rapturous applause from guests invited to its Tyseley Locomotive Works home and restoration base.

Moved into position on the works' turntable, the locomotive was officially recommissioned by the young family of Tyseley's works manager Alistair Meanley, son of its long-serving chief mechanical engineer Bob Meanley, who unveiled the Charles Collett-designed locomotive's nameplate. Throughout the day, *Clun Castle* steamed up and down the Tyseley demonstration line, double-heading with classmate No. 5043 *Earl of Mount Edgcumbe*.

The message was loud and clear. *Clun Castle* the legend was back, but it would not be until February 2019 that it would make its first comeback test runs on the national network, before proudly reclaiming a place in the heritage sector's main line steam fleet.

The history of *Clun Castle* has long been part of heritage railway folklore.

First allocated to Newton Abbot, it had a double chimney and a four-row superheater fitted in October 1959. Its biggest claim to fame was on May 9, 1964 on the Plymouth to Bristol leg of the 'Ian Allan Plymouth to Paddington' special, marking the unofficial 102.3mph record set 60 years earlier by GWR 4-4-0 *City of Truro* on Wellington Bank. This time round, *Clun Castle* was officially timed at 96mph on the descent of Wellington Bank.

Last shedded by British Railways at Gloucester in May 1965, it hauled the final official steam train out of Paddington (to Banbury) on June 11, 1965. When it was officially withdrawn

in December 1965, it was believed to be the last operating Castle.

In 1967, Pat Whitehouse, one of the founders of the Talyllyn Railway Preservation Society – which in effect launched the operational heritage railway movement – bought GWR 4-6-0 No. 4079 *Pendennis Castle* from enthusiast Mike Higson, who had bought it following its performance on the same Ian Allan charter, during which the firebars had melted.

However, Pat owned it for only a week before he was asked by the seller to retract his offer, as two other enthusiasts – multi-millionaire construction company supremo Bill McAlpine and his friend John Gretton – had made a higher bid.

Gentleman Pat readily agreed, but then his attention was brought to another of the Castles on that headline-grabbing 1964 trip – No. 7029.

After *Clun Castle* toured throughout England to mark the end of steam, in 1967 Pat and fellow Dart Valley

LEFT: On February 28, 2019, WR 4-6-0 No. 7029 *Clun Castle* storms through the classic GWR station at Hagley during its first public main line trip since passing its loaded test runs following its overhaul at Tyseley Locomotive Works. It was heading a Vintage Trains evening dining train from Birmingham Moor Street to Worcester and back. JOHN TITLOW

Railway director John Evans made up the shortfall in a fund which had been set up to buy No. 7029, transferring the locomotive to a new company, 7029 Clun Castle Ltd. BR sold it for the scrap value of £3600.

Both *Clun Castle* and *Pendennis Castle* were used on specials in the first weekend of March 1967 to mark the closure of Birmingham Snow Hill and the GWR main line from there to Birkenhead.

Pat negotiated storage for *Clun Castle* at Tyseley shed. It is thanks to him that the 1908-built steam depot, which was opened by the GWR as a result of expanding operations in the West Midlands, particularly the opening of the North Warwickshire Line as a new main line from Birmingham via Stratford-upon-Avon and Cheltenham to Bristol and the West Country, then developed a preservation identity of its own over and above its use as temporary storage for stock for the nascent Dart Valley Railway (now the South Devon Railway), the founding of which he was also heavily involved in.

Clun Castle stands proudly on the Tyseley Locomotive works turntable for its official relaunch into traffic on October 28, 2017. ROBIN JONES

In October 1968, No. 7029 Clun Castle Ltd also bought LMS Jubilee class 4-6-0 No. 5593 *Kolhapur*, and its supporters established the Standard Gauge Steam Trust as an educational charity.

The trust acquired a long-term lease on much of the Tyseley site, and established the Tyseley Collection. The site became Birmingham Railway Museum, which later became rebranded Tyseley Locomotive Works. In October 1968, two months after the end of BR steam haulage, Tyseley held its first, and very successful, open day.

In 1972, No. 7029 joined in the 'Return to Steam' tours after BR relaxed its post-1968 steam ban. *Clun Castle* was seen throughout England in the 1970s and 80s hauling steam railtours, and took a leading role in the 1985 GWR

In in early days in preservation, No. 7029 *Clun Castle* arrives at Birmingham Snow Hill. Its saviour Patrick Whitehouse, founder of what is now Tyseley Locomotive Works, is seen leaning out of the cab. DEREK PHILLIPS

LEFT: *Clun Castle* project manager Alistair Meanley and his children Emily and Tilly unveil the nameplate to declare No. 7029 back in traffic on October 28, 2017. ROBIN JONES

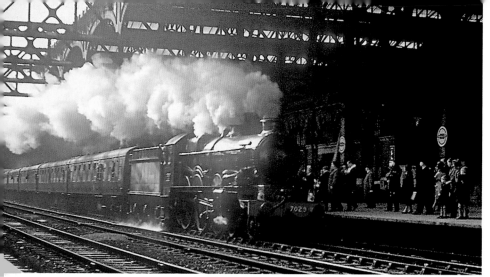

Clun Castle stands inside the old Birmingham Snow Hill station in the late 1960s with a northbound special. DEREK PHILLIPS

150 celebrations, taking daily shuttles between Gloucester and Swindon.

After a major overhaul, it emerged in British Railways livery in 1985. The following year, it hauled the last train from the old Birmingham Moor Street station prior to remodelling into its present format.

Until now, the locomotive was last seen on the main line in 1988, and afterwards visited heritage lines. Pat Whitehouse died in 1993, and his daughter Maggy, an Independent Catholic cleric who blessed the recommissioned locomotive at the above mentioned 2017 relaunch ceremony, told the assembled crowd Pat's ashes were thrown into the firebox of *Clun Castle* during a visit to the Great Central Railway in 1994.

Before that, *Clun Castle* had last steamed at Tyseley Locomotive Works in 2001, and its overhaul began in 2010.

Pat's son Michael, now chairman of Vintage Trains, told the assembled crowd: "Tyseley and all we do would never have happened if *Clun Castle* had not come here."

He thanked Birmingham railwaymen Bernard Rainbow, Phil Gloster and Colin Jacks, Tyseley's first volunteers, who all attended the relaunch.

When the fireman of the return train from Birkenhead to Snow Hill in March 1967 fell ill, Bernard was a passenger on the trip and stepped into the breach, Michael told the crowd. He subsequently led the volunteer movement at Tyseley, which looked after No. 7029 for 25 years on the main line. He also praised Alistair Meanley and his team for the standard of the restoration.

In so many ways, Tyseley Locomotive Works has replaced Swindon as the 'GWR hub' of the national network, having overhauled and operated so many of its steam-era products from there, and continues to do so.

BACK ON THE MAIN LINE AT LAST

Once the necessary equipment to comply with modern operating requirements on the national network had been fitted, *Clun Castle* was ready for its all-important test runs.

The first took place on Tuesday, February 19, 2019, when it ran light engine along the goods loop line from Tyseley to Bordesley, followed by a second light engine return run from Tyseley to Whitlock's End Halt on the North Warwickshire Line and back, and an evening loaded run with six coaches to Stratford-upon-Avon and back.

Two days later, it ran two round trips to Stratford, again outwards tender first along the North Warwickshire Line via Shirley and Henley-in-Arden and back via Claverdon, Hatton Junction and Lapworth, on the Birmingham to Leamington route. On the latter line, it was able to reach 82mph between Dorridge and Solihull, fulfilling its requirement to demonstrate it could do the maximum steam line speed of 75mph plus 10%, and in doing so surprised many commuters waiting at Solihull as it passed through.

A fourth day of main line test trips took place on February 26, this time with a very special VIP guest on board, in the form of 94-year-old Leo Leeney, who had helped build the boiler of *Clun Castle* at Swindon in 1950.

During his five years with the Royal Engineers, Leo served a three-year apprenticeship as a boilersmith at none other than Swindon Works. Yet he never told his wife Valerie or their daughters Bev and Lisa about the years he helped make railway history. His secret came out only when he read the *Daily Mail* on September 18, 2018. It contained a story about Vintage Trains launching its public share issue to become a Train Operating Company, accompanied by

WR 4-6-0 No. 7029 *Clun Castle* at Chester General before hauling the return 'Zulu' to Birmingham Snow Hill on March 4, 1967, marking the end of the GWR through route from the second city to Birkenhead. 8474TIM*

Flanked by footplate crew Alistair Meanley (left) and driver Ray Churchill, Leo Leeney, who helped build *Clun Castle's* boiler, stands alongside the locomotive at Stratford-upon-Avon during its February 28, 2019 loaded test run. ROBIN JONES

Rush hour traffic is no problem for a GWR-designed Castle 4-6-0, in the form of No. 7029 *Clun Castle*, as it crosses the M42, south of Widney Manor station in Solihull, with its February 21, 2019 loaded test run, returning to its Tyseley base. ROBIN COOMBES/VT

a picture of *Clun Castle*. "That's my locomotive," exclaimed an excited Leo, who now lives in Hodge Hill, Birmingham.

Bev contacted Vintage Trains to see whether it would be possible to visit the locomotive. In short, Leo and his devoted family were invited to not only see *Clun Castle* in steam but to board its penultimate loaded test run and tour Tyseley works.

Testing over, *Clun Castle* was given the green light to work its first main line charters in more than three decades.

On February 28 and March 7, No. 7029 hauled two evening dining trains from Birmingham Moor Street to Worcester, before Vintage Trains rostered it for its 2019 schedule of public charter trains.

Those diners marked the start of a new era, for the Vintage Trains Community Benefit Society share offer had by then raised more than £1million towards setting up Britain's newest Train Operating Company, with *Clun Castle* as its flagship, all ready for more chapters in the story of a Brunswick green legend to be written.

RIGHT: The earlier of two loaded test runs on February 26, 2019 saw *Clun Castle* stop at Birmingham's Acock's Green station to allow passengers to disembark. ROBIN JONES

Chapter 15

Purely by magic:

THE HALL THAT BECAME A CASTLE

Great Western Railway 4-6-0 No. 5972 *Olton Hall* was just another run-of-the-mill and not particularly remarkable member of its class, and might so easily have been cut up for scrap. Yet in the 21st century, its worldwide fame and legendary status at times eclipsed even that of *Flying Scotsman*, especially among the younger generation, and it was all down to a teenage wizard called Harry Potter.

No. 5972 *Olton Hall* was built at Swindon in 1937 and named after a mansion in a suburb of Solihull. It was one of a class of 330 versatile mixed-traffic locomotives designed by Charles Collett for the GWR.

They were operated all over the former Great Western system (and in BR days some way off it), and were equally at home on semi-fast or stopping passenger trains, express parcels or freight work.

No. 5972 was initially based at Neath and then allocated to Carmarthen until 1951, working throughout South Wales and as far afield as Bristol and Gloucester.

Following a brief spell at Plymouth, No. 5972 spent the next three years in the West Midlands, principally allocated to the predominantly freight shed of Oxley, Wolverhampton.

Olton Hall returned to the West Country in 1954 and worked a wide variety of trains, while based at Truro, Penzance and Plymouth, notably being recorded on 'The Cornishman' express on several occasions.

Returning to South Wales in 1959,

No. 5972 was allocated to Severn Tunnel Junction and Neath, before being withdrawn from Cardiff East Dock shed at the end of 1963, and subsequently sold for scrap to Woodham Bros, at Barry.

Here, owner Dai Woodham's philosophy was unique among the scrapyards which took delivery of withdrawn main line steam locomotives and cut them up within days.

He took the commercial decision that the scrapping of redundant railway wagons turned in a far quicker profit, so he left the locomotives he bought lined up in sidings, rusting away in the salty air of the Severn estuary, as a future investment for the day when there were no more wagons to cut up.

In the meantime, history records 213 former main line steam engines were saved for preservation purposes from his yard, and one of these was *Olton Hall*.

No. 5972 was bought privately for preservation in May 1981 – the 125th locomotive to be saved from Barry scrapyard – and taken to Procor (UK) Ltd's works at Horbury Junction, near Wakefield, for initial restoration. However, final restoration work was

GWR 4-6-0 No. 5972 *Olton Hall* in its guise as *Hogwarts Castle* waits at York station with West Coast Railway's 'Scarborough Spa Express' on June 2, 2004. The special coincided with the nearby National Railway Museum's Railfest 2004 event to mark the 200th anniversary of Richard Trevithick's first public display of a steam railway locomotive, and a century since *City of Truro's* unofficial 102.3mph run. ROBIN JONES

carried out at train operator West Coast Railways' depot at Carnforth, Lancashire, and the locomotive first steamed there in 1997.

Following completion of work in 1998, No. 5972's main line proving runs were made to Preston and Carlisle, before a short period of hire to the North Yorkshire Moors Railway.

No. 5972's main line passenger debut was not until May 22, 1999. This was because of gauging problems over non-former GWR lines in the north of

England, where clearances were much restricted. Indeed, the run was a surprise to observers, for few outside West Coast realised it was going to happen, many still believing that the locomotive was still under restoration at a shed in Wakefield

Olton Hall had been restored to BR lined passenger green livery and stepped in as a last-minute replacement for Stanier 8F No. 48151, hauling a seven-coach return trip over the Settle and Carlisle line.

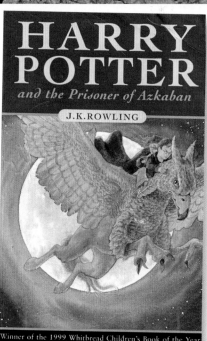

BELOW: The headboard carried by No. 5972 *Olton Hall* (aka *Hogwarts Castle*) at the Warner Brothers Studio Tour London in Leavesden, Hertfordshire. WBST

TOP and ABOVE: GWR 4-6-0 No. 5972 *Olton Hall* as *Hogwarts Castle* heads the 'Hogwarts Express' over the spectacular 100ft-high Glenfinnan Viaduct on the West Highland extension on February 22, 2003, during filming of J K Rowling's third Harry Potter novel, Harry Potter and the Prisoner of Azkaban. ROBIN JONES

Before the magic wand was waved: GWR 4-6-0 in BR Brunswick Green livery passes a snowbound Selside, between Settle and Ribblehead, with a northbound Hellifield to Carlisle and back Christmas shoppers' special on December 4, 2000. JOHN SHUTTLEWORTH

WHEN MAGICIANS EMBRACED VICTORIAN TRANSPORT TECHNOLOGY

Olton Hall was certainly another very welcome addition to the heritage-era main line steam fleet, but only at the time of its debut, no more than that. However, supernatural forces were to come into play and change its fortunes forever.

British author Joanne Rowling, who was born in Yate, Gloucestershire, was working as a researcher and bilingual secretary for Amnesty International when she dreamed up the idea for a story about a boy wizard called Harry Potter…while idling away the time on a delayed train from Manchester to London in 1990.

Her first Harry Potter novel in a series, which eventually extended to seven volumes, was Harry Potter and the Philosopher's Stone, published on June 26, 1997.

Published under the name J K Rowling, the novels outline the adventures of Harry and his friends Hermione Granger and Ron Weasley, who are students at Hogwarts School of Witchcraft and Wizardry, and who are locked in combat against the dark wizard Lord Voldemort, who seeks immortality and mastery over all other wizards and 'muggles' (non-wizarding people). The Harry Potter books were an instant hit with the public, attracting worldwide critical acclaim.

In short, they made the author, who had at the outset lived on state benefits, into the world's first billionaire author.

She is Britain's best-selling living author, with book sales exceeding £238 million, and as at February 2018, had sold more than 500 million copies worldwide, being translated into 80 languages. Her last four novels consecutively set records as the fastest-selling books in history, with the seventh volume selling around 11 million copies in the USA within 24 hours of its release.

In the story, the School of Witchcraft and Wizardry in Hogwarts Castle had

J K Rowling at the White House in April 2010. DANIEL OGREN*

been in existence for centuries. In days of yore, students would arrive on broomsticks, or on enchanted carts or carriages, on the backs of mythical magical creatures, or by use of a 'portkey', an object enchanted to instantly bring anyone touching it to a specific location.

However, the development of the steam locomotive in the days of Trevithick and the Stephensons did not go unnoticed. When in 1827 – two years before Stephenson's Rocket won the Rainhill Trials – Ottaline Gambol became Minister for Magic.

She looked at the non-magical transport technology that was taking shape at the time, and decided a steam locomotive would be a more secure and comfortable alternative to portkeys or other weird and wonderful means of getting to the castle. So, 19th-century engineers at Crewe were commissioned to build a locomotive to haul what would become known as the Hogwarts Express. This is the name of the train that makes a run between London King's Cross Platform 9¾ and Hogsmeade station, which serves the castle and its school.

The express makes its journey no fewer than six times a year, taking students to and from Hogwarts School of Witchcraft and Wizardry at the start and end of every term. It leaves Platform 9¾ on time at 11am each September 1 and arrives at its destination in the early evening.

'HOGWARTS EXPRESS' BECOMES A REALITY

Among the rows of rusting hulks that once ruled the roost on Britain's national network, but were slowly falling into decay in Barry scrapyard, was 1946-built Southern Railway Bulleid West Country light Pacific No. 34027 *Taw Valley*.

It was withdrawn from service at Salisbury in 1964 and given a second lease of life in 1980 when it was bought by enthusiast and engineer Bert Hitchen, and moved to the North Yorkshire Moors Railway for its restoration to begin, later being transferred to the East Lancashire Railway.

Restored to full working order, like *Olton Hall*, it was registered to run on the national network again, becoming a regular performer during the 1990s.

Taw Valley was repainted from green to full maroon livery with 'Hogwarts Express' nameplates following use at a previous low-key Harry Potter book launch at King's Cross station in 2000. As such, it toured parts of the country promoting the latest Harry Potter volume, to huge crowds of wizarding fans, who enjoyed book-signings by J K Rowling on the train.

By then the phenomenal popularity of the books had come to the attention of Hollywood, and Warner Brothers began planning a first movie to cash in on the worldwide success.

It was suggested *Taw Valley* could be used as the locomotive hauling the train

Hogwarts Castle waits at the head of the 'Hogwarts Express' on Platform 9¾ at King's Cross station in 2006. JAMES SHUTTLEWORTH

Olton Hall as *Hogwarts Castle* takes a pause between Warner Brothers' movie filming at Glenfinnan station on February 22, 2003. ROBIN JONES

The 'Hogwarts Express' near the front of Hogsmeade station in the Wizarding World of Harry Potter, which spans the Universal Orlando Resort in Florida. At the venue, you can buy an explorer ticket and pass through Platform 9¾ to board the 'Hogwarts Express' from King's Cross station in London, located inside Universal Studios Florida theme park, and travel to Hogsmeade station, situated inside Universal's Islands of Adventure theme park, next door to Universal Studios. HARSH LIGHT*

in the first film of the series. However, the film's director Chris Columbus dismissed the idea as No. 34027 looked far too modern as a steam engine.

Instead, No. 5972 *Olton Hall* was chosen instead, and West Coast signed a deal with Warner Brothers for it to become an international movie star.

It was painted bright red and renamed *Hogwarts Castle*, and a rake of West Coast British Railways Mk1

maroon coaches was provided to make up the 'Hogwarts Express'.

In its film role, the locomotive carries a 'Hogwarts Express' headboard on the smokebox, featuring the Hogwarts school crest. The same emblem is featured as part of the Hogwarts Railways' emblem on the tender and carriages.

In the film, the locomotive retains GWR number 5972, but has *Hogwarts*

Southern Railway Bulleid West Country light Pacific No. 34027 *Taw Valley* was repainted from green livery into maroon in 2000 to publicise the Harry Potter books, and is seen here during a visit to the Great Central Railway at Loughborough that year. However, the movie makers considered a Bulleid Pacific to be too 'modern' to represent *Hogwarts Castle* on the big screen.

RIGHT: No. 5972 *Olton Hall* as *Hogwarts Castle* waits to depart from Toddington station on the Gloucestershire Warwickshire Railway on May 19, 2009. IAN CROWDER

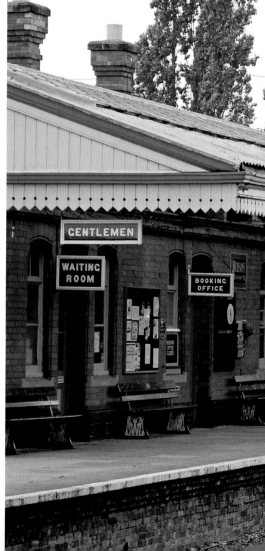

Castle nameplates, replacing those of *Olton Hall*.

No. 5972 appeared in the first session of filming at Goathland – which doubles up as Hogsmeade station – on the North Yorkshire Moors Railway, in September 2000.

The West Highland Extension between Fort William and Mallaig, with its spectacular Glenfinnan Viaduct, has been famously used for film sequences involving the 'Hogwarts Express', and accordingly has become a major tourist magnet in its own right. Scenes have also been filmed at Rannoch Moor, in the West Highlands.

Much location filming was subsequently undertaken at King's Cross using the 'Hogwarts Express' train, which arrived, of course, via the East Coast Main Line.

Platform 4 was used for the secret Platform 9¾, which only wizards can see. Trains packed with extras stood at platforms 3 and 5 during the filming.

The real platforms 9 and 10 are located in the 'commuter' station on the west side, but J K Rowling intended Platform 9¾ to be inside the original Lewis Cubitt-designed part of the station. The film follows her wishes in this respect.

Afterwards, a Platform 9¾ was

An artist's impression of passengers boarding the 'Hogwarts Express' at Platform 9¾. CONCEPT ART/WBST

erected on a wall near the platform. It has become one of London's most popular (and free) tourist attractions.

With the refurbishment of King's Cross in recent years, the Platform 9¾ sign has been moved to an enclave in the wall immediately to the east of the entrance at the King's Cross station complex.

It seems that every day, visitors are forever queuing up there to have their pictures taken by the sign.

The locomotive was also filmed on studio sets at Black Park, Slough, and Leavesden, Watford, taking a GWR Hall deeper into new territory.

In its decidedly non-authentic red livery, No. 5972 has now been seen on many parts of the UK rail network, in the distinctive Hogwarts red livery, appearing both as *Olton Hall* or, when on Hogwarts' duty, as *Hogwarts Castle*.

As well as visiting King's Cross several times, red-liveried No. 5972

A still from the movie Harry Potter and the Order of the Phoenix. WARNER BROTHERS

A regular sight at King's Cross: Regular queues of Harry Potter fans from all over the world waiting to have their picture taken by the Platform 9¾ sign. ROBIN JONES

has also worked excursions between Scarborough and York, as well as to Oxford, Stratford-upon-Avon and Paddington.

In May 2009, it was moved temporarily to the Gloucestershire Warwickshire Railway, and in July 2009 it was based at Tyseley Locomotive Works for use on some of the regular 'Shakespeare Express' trains run by Vintage Trains during the summer.

No. 5972 returned to the Gloucestershire Warwickshire Railway during its annual Wizard's Weekend event in 2010.

In late-2011 the locomotive was on static display in London's Hyde Park, in its 'Hogwarts' red livery, and in June-July 2014 it worked two final 'Wizards Express' rail tours from Manchester to York before its mainline certificate expired.

Needing a major overhaul, a deal was signed for it to be placed on static display from 2015 onwards at the Warner Bros Studio Tour, at Leavesden, where

Climb aboard the 'Hogwarts Express' carriage on Platform 9¾ at Warner Brothers Studio Tour London – The Making of Harry Potter. WBST

much of the Harry Potter filming was undertaken.

In 2010, a full-size and amazingly accurate wooden mock-up of No. 5972 *Hogwarts Castle* appeared at the new Wizarding World of Harry Potter theme park in Orlando, Florida. That venue has a total of three *Hogwarts Castle* replicas, two as part of the 'Hogwarts Express' train ride, with the other being a static exhibit in the Hogsmeade station area.

There are also static models at the other Wizarding World of Harry Potter locations in Hollywood and Japan.

Flying Scotsman is still considered to be the world's most famous locomotive, but how many full-size replicas of it are there around the globe?

The modern-day journey of *Olton Hall* in so many ways mirrors that of J K Rowling – true-life rags to riches stories that in most other situations belong to the realm of fantasy.

BUY A MODEL HALL - GET A CASTLE!

MODELMAKER Hornby issued an OO-gauge model of *Olton Hall* as *Hogwarts Castle* in the wake of the colossal commercial success of the Harry Potter books and film.

A GWR Hall is a smaller locomotive type than a Castle – with the red-liveried Hornby model being a Castle in disguise! The company has since produced new tooling for a Hall.

Hornby was not the only manufacturer to have made the same mistake: Märklin used a Castle in its 'Hogwarts Express' set. Hornby righted the ship in its Railroad range GWR 4-6-0 *Olton Hall* in 2015.

But who really cares: the 'Hogwarts Express' brought many a Christmas train set back under the Christmas tree for countless youngsters worldwide, who would never have thought to count the rivets to check for class accuracy!

Hornby 'Hogwarts Express' train set Harry Potter and the Half-Blood Prince, complete with DCC Sound. HORNBY

LNWR King George the Fifth

A PAST LEGEND FOR THE FUTURE

Recent decades have seen remarkable strides made in engineering in the heritage sector, not only in locomotive restoration but in the building of new ones from scratch, to re-create the legends that once were, but sadly have long since gone to the scrapyard. One of the latest such schemes to be making steady progress is that of building from scratch a new London & North Western Railway George the Fifth 4-4-0, one that has already been aptly bestowed with a royal name.

TOP: LNWR George the Fifth 4-4-0 No. 2124 *John Rennie* climbing Camden Bank. LNWR KGVSLT

RIGHT: LNWR George the Fifth 4-4-0 No. 2494 *Perseus* at Llandudno Junction c1924. LNWR KGVSLT

Cecil J Allen wrote that the LNWR George the Fifth was the finest 4-4-0 to grace Britain's railways until Maunsell's Schools class came along 20 years later.

Charles Bowen Cooke, chief mechanical engineer of the LNWR, developed the George the Fifth class as one of several responses to the ever-increasing demand for faster journeys containing more passengers, together with 'meals on wheels' and other creature comforts.

Cooke developed former locomotive superintendent George Whale's Precursor design of 1904, which itself has been described as an enlarged Webb 'Jumbo' 2-4-0. The Precursor made a tremendous impression, hauling fast heavy expresses, despite its small size.

Cooke was appointed as LNWR chief mechanical engineer on March 1, 1909, a few months after Whale retired. Cooke was an operating man but one with great interest in the application of the scientific developments of the time as applied to locomotive design at home

and abroad. He consulted Dr Schmidt, a leading figure in the development of superheating. Schmidt's recommendations included long-travel piston valves and high superheat.

Regrettably, they also included Schmidt's wide piston ring, a single wide ring that required a great deal of painstaking skilled fitting to assemble, and suffered excessive wear and leakage at higher mileages. This was ironic, as the far superior standard narrow piston ring was developed at Crewe in 1852 by John Ramsbottom. It took 20 years to fit narrow rings and eliminate this weakness.

Cooke built 20 locomotives based on the well-proven Precursor, altering only where necessary for the superheater and piston valves. Valve travel was very long for the time, being only ¼in less than that of an A4 Pacific! Steam temperatures of 650°F were claimed.

The build was split: 10 of the Queen Mary class with piston valves but saturated, and 10 George the Fifth class with piston valves and superheaters. Cooke fitted the first of each build with an adjustable cone between blast pipe and petticoat to determine the final nozzle size. From the summer of 1910 these two types were put to work on the same duties and monitored in a true comparative test. Both demonstrated improvements on the Precursor's performance, but superheating was found to reduce coal consumption by a quarter, a massive saving in fuel costs.

The saturated Queen Mary class was superheated, and building of Georges continued until 1915. Conversion of 130 Precursors to George standard started in 1913, and continued until 1926, effectively adding to the fleet of 90 Georges. The firemen appreciated the deep firebox of the Precursor and the George, being easy to fire with a round of eight shovelfuls to make a fire more than 2ft deep. They particularly liked the George for having a quarter less coal to shift, as well as Cooke's 'married man's tender', with its sloping bunker and higher shovelling plate.

The boiler had an excellent stream

The first visit by a reigning British monarch to a railway workshop took place on April 21, 1913. Class members Nos. 2663 *George the Fifth* and 1800 Coronation arrive at Crewe Works with King George V and Queen Mary on board. LNWR KGVSLT

circuit, and steamed consistently well. It could produce 20,000lb of steam an hour at full pressure against both injectors, helped by the excellent design of the front end, with its chimney almost as good as the much later Lempor. Crewe boilermakers were top class, as William Stanier later acknowledged.

The impact of such a small engine handling heavy trains at express speeds was enormous. On the Birmingham two-hour trains of 400 tons they set a benchmark lasting for the rest of the steam era. Train timing enthusiasts recorded many astounding feats.

Cecil J Allen recorded (*The Railway Magazine*, January 1912) what came to be regarded as the gold standard for the class when *Wild Duck* stalled on Camden Bank with the 10.30am from Euston, booked non-stop to Crewe in 171 minutes. From being 11 minutes late at Willesden, the engine whisked its 410-ton train to Crewe, a two-minute early arrival thwarted only by a signal check at Crewe. Author OS Nock demonstrated this apparently outstanding run was in fact little out of the ordinary. Railway locomtive expert and author William

Alfred Tuplin ranked it as No. 3 in a table of outstanding performance of pre-grouping locomotives.

On the Northern Division, the Georges replaced Experiment 4-6-0s, an unusual event. However, even on the mountain section the Georges improved performance. Sometimes the near-impossible was attempted, as when *Saddleback* took a 460-ton train over the 91 miles from Preston to Carlisle in a total time of 116 minutes, despite signal checks.

A human perspective is given in The *Railway Magazine*, September 1957, narrated by an un-named fireman. He tells the story of a run on the 6pm Euston-Liverpool, 460 tons non-stop to Edge Hill, due at 9.28pm. The engine and crew would have come up on the 11am from Lime Street the same bleak windy day. There is plenty of banter between fireman and the driver, Paddy, to suggest a good working relationship.

Starting with such a heavy train required good preparation: setting sand down as they back onto the train, warming the cylinders front and back, and building the fire to full temperature with the dart and the blower. Given the

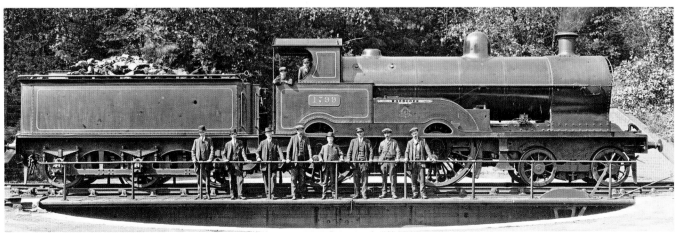

LNWR George the Fifth 4-4-0 No. 1799 *Woodcock* on the turntable at Bletchley in 1917. LNWR KGVSLT

A LEGEND LOST – TO BE FOUND AGAIN?

Enthusiast Bruce Nixon wrote in the railway press urging a new-build George, which chimed with like-minded Paul Hibberd's efforts to assess the feasibility. Contact was made, and the George the Fifth Steam Locomotive Trust was formed in 2012.

Key players were Tom Mainprize, a graduate member involved at Didcot Railway Centre, and a volunteer with Princess Coronation Pacific No. 6233 *Duchess of Sutherland;* Jamie Keyte-Smith, engineering director of Derbyshire firm Keyte Smith Ltd, who also gives the benefit of his professional expertise; and Peter Stanton, another professional engineer.

The first part made was the smokebox door.

The trust was granted permission to name the locomotive *Prince George*, subject to the condition the name be bestowed on the prince's first birthday, July 22, 2014. A section of lower cab side and splasher was made and expertly painted by Heritage Painting in time for the naming ceremony.

The trust now has a full smokebox with chimney, mounted on a stand with the front buffer beam and footplating. Other parts made are the front-end frame plates, the coupling rod forgings, the bogie wheel pattern, the dome pattern, and the dome cover itself.

The trust intends to re-create the atmosphere of early 20th century rail travel as far as possible. However, a replica involves some compromise, legislation changes, public expectations change, technology, and industry change.

The building of new Peppercorn A1 Pacific No. 60163 *Tornado* demonstrated that main line new build steam is possible, if conformance is considered from the first.

The Rail Safety and Standards Board updated the Heritage Standards in December 2017, and the trust's team attended the joint Office of Rail & Road/RSSB roadshow at the National Railway Museum in December 2018, and found it very useful. The trust has contracted certification body Ricardo Rail, and its first submission for the coupling rods has been approved.

Behind the scenes a great deal of what might be classed as set-up work has been going on. For instance, the trust has most of the all-important original drawings, in an online repository.

Design work continues, at present concentrated on the boiler. A single water gauge, as originally fitted, is unacceptable – a second gauge was fitted in later years. The connection to the main steam pipe would seem to require a disposable apprentice to wriggle into the boiler through the dome. These two items must be changed.

A riveted boiler is possible, but would prompt the question: Why? It is slower to build, more complex and expensive. A welded boiler requires no change of appearance and does the same job.

Other new-build projects have stuck with the fully authentic riveted boiler, but the trust's decision to have a welded boiler is based on practicality. Industry today doesn't rivet, it welds, whereas a century ago welding was untried in pressure vessels.

Another aspect is the internal design of the boiler, tubes and superheaters. Cooke had little ability to carry out the calculations to optimise the layout: a modern laptop in the hands of a skilled engineer is a powerful tool.

Expert advice is that fitting 28 rather than the LNWR 24 superheater elements in larger flues, with maybe about half the original number of small tubes, will give even hotter steam than the original.

This seems like a good thing, so the trust hopes to implement this change: this is important because every extra bit of power will help with main line pathing, and hopefully ease the trust's path to hauling trains of a decent length with more earning capacity.

As may be imagined, the boiler has to be reviewed against rigorous standards, and while this could be left to the Certification Body, not only would it greatly increase their costs, it would also risk expensive late design changes.

Detailed work on the boiler reveals much about the inter-relationship between its different elements. Sometimes it pays to make haste slowly.

The trust intends to order at least the boiler barrel with its dome plinth and mudhole in 2019.

The front end of the new LNWR George the Fifth 4-4-0 *Prince George*. LNWR KGVSLT

right-away the crew and steed blasted away up Camden bank.

It was flat out all the way to Tring up relatively easy gradients, and little easier on to Rugby because of the gale.

Such was the quality of the LNWR main line that Rugby was the first significant check on speed. It was more of the same to Stafford except when Paddy shut off for a distant signal that was on and the fire blew back. Both men dived for the blower, and there was no harm done, but Paddy got told they are better off without a blowback – probably in language to turn the air blue.

Paddy sees the Stafford station clock showing they are about five minutes late, and announces they will need to get a move on. After more banter, Paddy volunteers to fire for a while. Sparks fly up to Whitmore, and gravity helps them on to Crewe, where they are still slightly late. Paddy was bent on right time at Edge Hill and took up the shovel again.

Weaver Junction was the next slack, followed by a steepish Birdswood bank. The engine still steamed, but was slogging hard against gradient and wind. By Runcorn our fireman retires to the tender for the rest of the trip, his coal seat a mere couple of hundredweight by this time. He tells Paddy that if more coal is needed, he will have to put it on himself.

The last few miles thin the fire down, causing lots of sparks from the chimney. Arrival at Edge Hill is a minute or two late, and its crew are relieved there.

This story shows how a small engine could do a job needing continuous high-power output for several hours on end.

Then came the catastrophe of the First World War, followed by the Grouping of 1923. LNWR passenger locomotives initially spread their sphere of action to bolster LMS services off their own lines, but then gradually fell from favour. An unwise decision to remove the crank centre bearing and framing was followed by a plague of cracked frames.

By the outbreak of the Second World War, there were very few LNWR passenger locomotives left. Survivors kept going through the war, but in 1949, the last George – *Sirocco*, actually a superheated Precursor – was lined up with the last Prince and final Claughton to be photographed before cutting up.

STEAMING AHEAD

What of the future? The trust is hoping to support an undergraduate's year in industry, if the application is approved. The project will be to review loadings in the bogie wheel, and make any necessary changes to support its use.

In effect, this means the wheels, tyre and axle, as these affect the wheel design, and it makes sense to invest a relatively small amount of extra work to complete the design and seek

Bending the handrail to shape around the front of the new locomotive.
LNWR KGVSLT

The nameplate and splasher of the new locomotive. LNWR KGVSLT

The steam dome as seen on April 24, 2019. RENS DELROSSO

its certification. Then the trust can progress to the bogie design itself.

With the front end completed for display purposes, it would make sense to consider creating a CAD model for the cylinder block casting – a big-ticket item.

There are options to be considered here, whether to cast it as originally made, or fabricate it. The trust could then fit its front frame plates to the block and permanently assemble it to its display front. That would free resources to restart the trust's analysis of the Joy valve gear, to assess the forces involved. A big spreadsheet exists, but needs work to deliver results.

Why does this matter when the trust does not intend to order motion parts in the immediate future? To determine its forces on the connecting rod, hence

its forces on the crank axle to confirm the axle box size. In other words, it will enable the trust to move ahead with the rear main frames and the locomotive erection process.

In the meantime, there will be many smaller items which can be progressed. For instance, the front buffer beam will require a vacuum pipe, buffers (strengthened, maybe with an Oleo core. J M Dunne said LNWR buffers 'snapped like carrots').

Then there are the draw hook and front dragbox (also modified: modern traction could inflict damage and the first locomotives had rigidly mounted draw hooks, later ones a very limited resilient spring).

The upper cab design is progressing, so there is the possibility of fitting that

with the trust's splasher and lower cab to display the 'bodywork' of the full-length locomotive. The trust is now at a very exciting stage of the project, with major items coming along shortly, and ongoing design work will enable it to commission more manufacturing.

Soon, the trust will need a fixed base, preferably one with LNWR connections and readily accessible to its team.

* Would you like to help re-create the legend that was the LNWR George the Fifth class?
Contact Paul Hibberd, 62 High Street, Buntingford, Hertfordshire SG9 9AH.
Telephone 01763 272883 or email paulhibberd@gmail.com
Donations are welcome at:
newprincegeorgesteam.org.uk

Handrail knobs made for the new George the Fifth 4-4-0. LNWR KGVSLT

The forging of the coupling rod nearing the final operation at Somers forge in October 2017.

Chapter 17

Restored Union Pacific Railroad 4000 class Big Boy 4-8-8-4 No. 4014 – now the biggest operational steam locomotive in the world. UP

The biggest legend of them all is back AND IN STEAM!

Britain supplied the first steam railway locomotive to the United States in the form of the *Stourbridge Lion*. In May 2019, the Union Pacific Railroad returned one of the biggest of them all to steam to mark the 150th anniversary of the completion of the transcontinental railroad, and generating media headlines across the globe.

At 12.47pm on May 10, 1869, both American and global transport history was made, at Promontory Summit, 66 miles north-west of Salt Lake City, where the Central Pacific Railroad from the west was ceremonially joined to the Union Pacific Railroad (UP) from the east, to form what first became known as the Pacific Railroad, then the Overland Route and now First Transcontinental Railroad.

The Pacific Railway Act was signed in 1862 by President Abraham Lincoln, who came up with the idea of a transcontinental railroad to unite a bitterly divided nation, with the two companies granted land rights and finance to lay tracks.

The railroad was built using horses, oxen, hand carts, wagons and the toil of mainly Irish immigrants working on the line that came from the east, and mostly Chinese workers on the section that came from the west. They worked

around the clock, risking their lives by blasting through rocks with gunpowder and nitroglycerine and shovelling snow on high mountain peaks. Several hundred workers perished.

The completed route ran for 1912 miles between the eastern US rail network at Omaha, Nebraska/Council Bluffs, Iowa, to the Pacific coast at the Oakland Long Wharf on San Francisco Bay.

Built between 1863-69, it was the culmination of a stupendous feat of 19th-century engineering, which transformed

Big Boy, a giant 4-8-8-4 Mallet type engine, is 133 feet long, nearly one-half the length of a city block, weighs 1,208,750 pounds, and has a fuel capacity of 28 tons. This monster of the rails is hinged in the center to permit it to take curves it otherwise could not accomplish.

One Big Boy does the work which formerly required two locomotives, and when under full steam consumes 100,000 pounds of water and 22,000 pounds of coal per hour. It sets a world standard for size and power. Union Pacific Railroad has a large fleet of these giants in service.

From
Union Pacific Exhibit
CHICAGO RAILROAD FAIR
June 25 - October 2, 1949

A contemporary postcard view of Big Boy No. 4019 in action.
ROBIN JONES COLLECTION

LEFT: A souvenir postcard of Big Boy No. 4002 issued at the Chicago Railroad Fair in 1949.

the American West as the nation was emerging from the bloody Civil War, the end of a great race between the Central Pacific and Union Pacific Railroad companies to see who could get to the meeting spot first.

At that moment, when the two lines met, a golden spike was hammered home to join the final panels of track on either side, triggering the immediate sending of a telegraph to President Ulysses S Grant that contained a single word: D-O-N-E. It sparked national celebrations.

An explanatory telegram read: "The last rail is laid. The last spike is driven. The Pacific railroad is completed. The point of junction is 1086 miles west of the Missouri River and 690 miles east of Sacramento City."

The bells at Independence Hall in Philadelphia rang while 100 guns were fired in New York and American flags were hung in cities.

The completed railroad shortened cross-county travel from as long as six months in wagons and stagecoaches to about 10 days on the rails, and served as a unifying moment for the war-torn nation. Before the railroad was completed, the cost of travelling across the US was about $1000. The price dropped to around $150, thanks to the railroad.

The railroad also linked the US to the world, carrying products from Asia and Europe. The first freight shipment across the new railroad included casks of tea from Japan. It opened up new markets for both imported and exported goods. Its completion eradicated the concept of the 'frontier' and greatly accelerated Anglo-European settlement of the American West, which aligned it politically with the Union states of the north. However, it also hastened the demise of the Plains Indians, as well as the bison herds on which they depended.

The golden spike included the inscription: "May God continue the unity of our country as this railroad unites the two great oceans of the world."

The spikes were afterwards replaced with iron ones to stop them from being stolen.

AN EVEN GREATER EFFORT REQUIRED

However, 70 years after the First Transcontinental Railroad was completed the steep Rocky Mountains of Wyoming and Utah were still causing problems for UP despite its massive steam locomotives, which often had to be moved in multiple to take heavy freight trains over the unforgiving gradients.

The need was greatest in Utah's Echo Canyon, which became a bottleneck for busy transcontinental train traffic, especially at the outbreak of the Second World War when railroad activity intensified.

In 1940, UP engineers teamed up with the American Locomotive Company (ALCO) to build one of the world's largest steam locomotives, each weighing more than one million pounds, and were 132ft 9in long and weighed 1,200,000lbs. They were the UP 4000 class Big Boys.

Stood on its end, Big Boy would be the height of a 13-storey building, weighing more than a Boeing 747 fully loaded with passengers, and able to pull 16 Statues of Liberty over a mountain.

Minus the tender, the Big Boy has the longest engine body of any reciprocating steam locomotive. The type is also believed to comprise the heaviest steam locomotives built, at 1,208,750lbs for the engine and tender.

By today's standards, each Big Boy cost around $4.4million to construct.

Twenty-five Big Boys were built exclusively for Union Pacific. Because of their great length, the frames of the Big Boys were 'hinged' or articulated, to allow them to negotiate curves. They have a 4-8-8-4 wheel arrangement, which meant they had four wheels on the leading set of 'pilot' wheels, which guided the engine, eight drivers, another set of eight drivers, and four wheels following, which supported the rear of the locomotive.

They were designed to haul freight over the Wasatch mountains between Ogden, Utah and Green River, Wyoming. In the late Forties, they were reassigned to Cheyenne, Wyoming, where they hauled freight over Sherman Hill to Laramie, Wyoming.

According to a Union Pacific executive, the class was originally to have been called the 'Wasatch'. However, one day while one of the engines was being built, an unknown worker scrawled 'Big Boy' in chalk on its front – and so the legendary name was born.

As built, the Big Boys had large grates

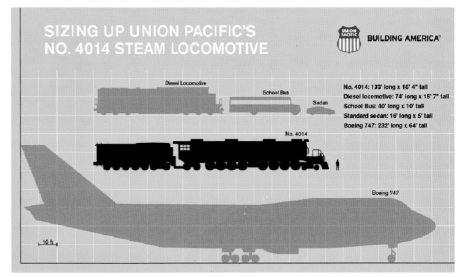

A comparison of the size of a Big Boy against a modern US diesel, motor car, school bus and a Boeing 747. UP

Big Boy No. 4014 and 'Living Legend' No. 844 face each other at Ogden Union station on May 9 for Union Pacific's own version of the 150th anniversary celebrations. COURTESY TRAINS MAGAZINE

Restored UP Big Boy No. 4014 arrives at Ogden Union station on May 9, 2019, for the start of celebrations to mark the 150th completion of the First Transcontinental Railroad. UP

Tapping a ceremonial golden spike between No. 4014 and No. 844 at Ogden Union station on May 9, 2019 are (left to right) Sandy Dodge, a descendent of General Grenville Dodge, Utah Governor; Gary Herbert, Union Pacific chairman; president and CEO Lance Fritz; Utah Congressman Rob Bishop; Margaret Yee; and Scott Moore, Union Pacific senior vice president corporate relations and chief administrative officer. Margaret Yee's ancestors were among thousands of Chinese immigrants who forged the transcontinental railroad for Central Pacific. General Dodge was a US Civil War veteran and Union Pacific's chief engineer during construction of the railroad. UP

to burn the low-quality bituminous coal from Union Pacific-owned mines in Wyoming.

As an experiment, No. 4005 was converted to burn oil, but failed because of uneven heating in the Big Boy's large, single-burner firebox.

Hailed as a defining pinnacle of steam locomotive design – and of course, light years ahead of the *Stourbridge Lion* – they were in so many ways to steam locomotive technology what the First Transcontinental Railroad had been to travel.

Big Boy No. 4014 was delivered to Union Pacific in December 1941. The locomotive was retired in December 1961, having travelled 1,031,205 miles in its 20 years in service. UP then donated it to the Railway and Locomotive Historical Society and the RailGiants museum in in Pomona, Southern California.

The last revenue-earning train hauled by a Big Boy ended its run early in the morning on July 21, 1959. Most were stored operational until 1961, and four remained in operational condition at Green River, Wyoming until 1962.

Eight of the Big Boys are preserved today.

In 2013, UP reacquired No. 4014 from the RailGiants Museum and took it back to its Cheyenne workshops to begin a restoration process, which has taken more than five years.

The aim is to have the sole operational class survivor taking part in a year of celebrations to mark the 150th anniversary of the completion of the First Transcontinental Railroad, starting this year.

The restoration involved the disassembly, inspection, and repair of every component, plus a conversion to oil burning – oil being easier to obtain than the coal it once burned.

Northern class 4-8-4 No. 844 (right) was built in 1944 and was the last steam locomotive built for Union Pacific. A high-speed passenger engine, it hauled named trains such as the 'Overland Limited', 'Los Angeles Limited', 'Portland Rose' and 'Challenger'. The Northerns were used by most large US railroads in dual passenger and freight service; UP had 45 of them. When diesels took over all of the company's passenger trains, No. 844 was switched to freight service in Nebraska between 1957-59. It was saved in 1960 from being scrapped and thankfully reserved for special trains. Hailed as UP's 'Living Legend', No. 844 is fabled among enthusiasts for its excursion runs, especially over the crossing of Sherman Hill, between Cheyenne and Laramie, Wyoming. It appeared at the 1981 opening of the California State Railroad Museum in Sacramento, the 1984 World's Fair in New Orleans, and the 50th anniversary celebration of Los Angeles Union station in 1989. Two other Northerns are on public display: No. 814 in Council Bluffs, Iowa and No. 833 in Ogden, Utah. A third, No. 838, is stored in Cheyenne as a source of spares for No. 844. UP

Even diehard enthusiasts thought it would be impossible to return a Big Boy to steam, not just because of their size, but also because of their mechanical complexity.

However, No. 4014 confounded such critics to the immense credit of the UP restoration team, and finally rolled out of the restoration shop in Cheyenne for a relaunch ceremony on Saturday, May 4, as hundreds watched. The cost of the restoration was estimated at around $4m, although UP has not confirmed any figure.

No. 4014 is now officially the largest operational steam locomotive in the world.

After leaving the workshop, it headed toward Utah for the start of the celebrations, with countless spectators lining the route and grabbing every vantage point, just as is so often the case with *Flying Scotsman* in the UK.

No. 4014 was unable to make it to the official Spike 150 festivities on May 10 at Promontory Summit. Having been removed as part of a Second World War scrap drive, there are no longer any tracks it could use to reach the windswept site of the Golden Spike National Historical Park, overlooking the Great Salt Lake.

Instead, Union Pacific arranged its own celebration on May 9 at Ogden's Union station, where No. 4014 re-enacted' the 1869 golden spike ceremony with Northern 4-8-4 'Living Legend' No. 844, the last steam locomotive built for UP, and which has remained in service since 1944.

After the UP ceremony, No. 4014 remained on display at Ogden for three days before it returned via Evanston, Wyoming, on its way back to Cheyenne. After that, it was pencilled in for a nationwide tour of 150th anniversary celebrations.

The words 'Big Boy' chalked on the smokebox door of No. 414 say it all! UP

East and West shaking hands after laying of the last rail of the first transcontinental railroad in 1869. UP

The 40-year-old replicas of original 'golden spike' locomotives No. 60 *Jupiter* and No. 119 are seen with an army of re-enactors who were re-staging the original ceremony from May 10, 1869 (150 years to the day) at Promontory Summit. COURTESY TRAINS MAGAZINE

REPLICAS IN 1869 REPLAY AT PROMONTORY SUMMIT

Friday, May 10, saw around 20,000 visitors swarm to the official Spike 150 celebration at Golden Spike National Historic Park. Some people came from as far as China, many decked out in 19th-century costume, to watch replicas of the two locomotives, which had featured in the original ceremony, take centre stage in the re-enactment, as music, bells and cannon fire rang out.

Central Pacific's No. 60 *Jupiter* and UP's No. 119, both 4-4-0s, were scrapped long ago (No. 119 in 1903 and *Jupiter* in 1909), but in 1974, the National Park Service approached O'Connor Engineering Laboratories of Costa Mesa, California, to construct exact, full-size replicas of both, after Walt Disney declined the job.

Because no original plans existed, more than 700 detailed engineering drawings were re-created, based almost entirely on photographs taken of the engines during the 1869 ceremony.

The pair were completed in 1979, and began operations on May 10 of that year, 110 years after the original Golden Spike ceremony, and continue to make demonstration runs, on a portion of restored track where the original ceremony was held.

On May 10, participants adopted similar poses for a series of photographs inspired by the original, after shiny replicas or the original gold and silver spikes were used, while *Jupiter* and No. 119 faced each other none to nose. Whistle blasts, hissing steam and clanging bells dominated the proceedings at the modern-day replay, before the sending of the original coast-to-coast telegraph bulletin was staged.

US Interior Secretary David Bernhardt said at the ceremony: "The story of this site says so much about our country.

"The joining of the two rail lines created a new sense of connectedness that helped form a common national identity."

The performance of a live musical re-creation of the 1869 ceremony followed, sparking a three-day festival of music, theatre and special exhibits at the park.

The celebrations marked an ultimate railway legend – not just of the return to steam of a Big Boy, something that few had ever dared hope for, but a reminder of the major part that steam and railroad played in both US and modern world history. Maybe, *Stourbridge Lion* has much to claim credit for!

Back in steam after nearly six decades: UP Big Boy No. 4104 steams again at the Cheyenne restoration workshop in April. UP